Going Home

By ROBERT A. RAINES

ROBERT A. RAINES

Going Home

Published in San Francisco by

HARPER & ROW, PUBLISHERS

New York Hagerstown San Francisco London

Acknowledgment is made for the permission of Charles
Scribner's Sons to reprint from "The Cardinals" in Notes
of an Alchemist by Loren Eiseley, copyright © 1972 by
Loren Eiseley; of Alfred A. Knopf, Inc., to reprint from
Changing by Liv Ullmann, copyright © 1976, 1977 by
Liv Ullmann; of Doubleday & Company, Inc., and of
Faber and Faber Ltd. to reprint "The Waking" and
portions of "The Longing," copyright © 1962 by
Beatrice Roethke as Administratrix of the Estate of
Theodore Roethke, from The Collected Poems of
Theodore Roethke.

FIRST EDITION

Designed by Jim Mennick

Library of Congress Cataloging in Publication Data

Raines, Robert Arnold.
    GOING HOME.

    1. Raines, Robert Arnold.   2. Christian
biography—United States.   I. Title.
BR1725.R25A33 1979   287'.632'0924 [B]
ISBN 0-06-066768-0   78-15834

79 80 81 82 83 10 9 8 7 6 5 4 3 2 1

To Roses, Dick, John,
and our parents

Contents

Preface

THIS BOOK is different from my previous books in its autobiographical character. I am trying here to understand and articulate my faith and life journey of the last nine years. It is not an easy thing to discern and disentangle. If the book seems self-centered, I hope it may rather be centered in the self. There is doubtless a mix of both in these pages. I ask your understanding.

I want to express my admiration, love, and gratitude for the members of my family who participated with me in the struggle of going home. I learned in my own experience that blood is thicker than water.

Thanks to my wife Cindy for living this journey with me and, in particular, for clear-eyed editing of the book. Thanks to Judy Holmes, my administrative assistant and friend, for her tireless good nature and craftsmanship in the typing of draft upon draft of this manuscript. Thanks also to my encouraging editors at Harper & Row, publishers of my first books, and, fittingly, of this one.

Thanks finally to the people and place of Kirkridge, where I have experienced acceptance, nurture, and friendship during the time of going home.

When I quote from the Bible I use the Revised Standard Version, unless it is otherwise noted.

Glen Arbor, Michigan

1 | *Apprehended*

By faith Abraham obeyed when he was called to go out to a place which he was to receive as an inheritance. . . .

Hebrews 11:8a

$\mathcal{I}N\ AUGUST$ 1970, I was on my way from my parish in Philadelphia to my new parish in Columbus, Ohio. En route I spent twelve days at a National Training Laboratory (NTL) in Bethel, Maine. I became a part of an encounter group of fourteen people that met several hours daily over a period of nearly two weeks. The group was a mixture of men and women of a variety of professions. I was the only clergyman. We began meeting on a Monday. Our room had chairs against the wall, a blackboard, and mats on the floor. I had been having my normally positive, successful time in that small group. Friday night at the end of the first week I happened to sit on one of the mats. At one point in the conversation a middle-aged psychiatric social worker who was a member of the group looked at me and said, "Bob, I can't tell whether you're sincere, whether you're for real." Someone else nodded and said, "You seem to smile the same way at everybody. Do you really feel that good all the time?"

The conversation moved on to another topic, but I felt a sore spot begin moving in me. After a few minutes I asked the others to come back and explore further with me that question about my sincerity. The group leader then suggested that each person give me, in one word, the way I came through to them. The leader started by giving me the word "accepting." Someone else gave me the word "sincere." A Jewish woman gave me the word "Wasp," which hurt my feelings because I hadn't felt I was coming through like that! Then a young woman said, "I don't want to hurt your feelings, but my word for you is 'patronizing.' I get the feeling that you think you've got the answer for my needs, but that you don't have needs, that it's a one-way street." The next person, a Canadian management trainer, said, "My word for you is 'paternal.' I feel you treat me like your son instead of your brother." Then a sixty-year-old college teacher asked, "When was the last time you said *no* to someone?" I couldn't remember. The last person, a community worker from a midwestern city, said, "I can't get it into one word. My phrase for you is 'All-American Christian.'" He grinned and said, "It's not *all* negative." Something was beginning to crumble inside me, although I still retained my composure.

The leader then suggested that the others go around the group again and give me, in one word, a gift. He started by giving me the gift of "latitude." A woman gave me the gift of "the ability to ask for help." Others gave me the gift of "choice," "freedom," "honesty." The college teacher gave me the gift of "the ability to say *no*." Another person was struggling to do right by me and finally said, "I've got to give you a gift in Yiddish." He said, "I want to give you the gift of 'Geschmacht.' It means 'salt' or 'tang' or 'earthiness.' It's the difference between soft white bread with the crusts cut off and pumpernickel!"

The meeting was soon over. I was on the mat pulling myself together when the first thing I knew, one of the group members was on her knees beside me hugging me. I had a few tears at that point. There were smiles and gestures of affirmation from other members, and then the people were gone. I went out for a long walk, wanting to remember those words and knowing that something valuable and threatening was happening to me. I returned from my walk to the community room where people from all the groups in the lab met after their individual meetings to eat, drink, and talk. I passed by a table where many people from my group were seated. I could feel love and warmth coming at me from them. I sat down, and in a gentle and kindly way they began to talk with me. "Why do you feel such an excessive sense of responsibility? Why do you want to please other people so much? Why can't you acknowledge your own needs?" As I received their grace and acceptance, all at once I felt I was going to cry. I hadn't cried in years, in decades. I can remember fighting it, neck muscles stiffening, until my jaw hit the top of the table, and heaving sobs rolled out of me. I was unable to control myself. It was as though I'd been damming up my tears for forty years and they wouldn't be contained any longer. The shaking, sobbing, and heaving were totally strange and appalling. Yet at the same time I had the sense that I was all right, that something good was happening to me. I became aware of arms and heads and words from others in the group and the sound of another man crying. And then a man across the table reached over to me and engaged me arm to arm and began to ask me questions, two of which I remember. He said, "What do you resent?" I heard myself saying, "I resent God for loading on me this burden of obligation. I resent my parents for laying this trip on me and the church for binding me into my role, and I resent myself for buying it all." And then he asked, "What do you appreciate?" I can remember feeling grateful he asked me that because I wanted to express warm feelings now, too. I was able to express my appreciation for the love of God, for my parents loving me the best way they knew how, for the church giving me a ministry, and for my own life. In a few more moments my heaving subsided. People left and I went back to my room to lie on my bed. For the next two hours, whenever my thoughts went back to the table, the heaving began again. I let it happen, wanting to experience as deeply as possible whatever was going on inside me.

What happened to me, in me, that night in Bethel? I've been living that question for nine years. It has taken me nine years to suffer, choose, and struggle my way through a painful transition to a new place of integrity and wholeness. In psychological terms, I got in touch with the shadow side of my being. Carl Jung speaks of the shadow side of the self as the repressed, hidden, unconscious parts of the self. Daniel Levinson, Yale psychologist, wrote that the critical question at midlife is the goodness of the fit between the self and the life structure.[1] One makes initial choices—marital, vocational, life style, value system, belief system—in one's twenties, and usually lives those choices into the thirties. Then in the late thirties or early forties one takes stock of what's happened and where one is regarding choices and the life structure he has built. Those parts of the self that have been denied or set aside in order to make it happen according to one's initial life plan

---

[1] Daniel Levinson, *The Seasons of a Man's Life* (New York: Knopf, 1978).

now swell up. Levinson illustrated this in the words of Truman Capote: "Those other voices in other rooms clamor to be heard." For me, those other voices were the voices of anger, grief, and sexual energy.

I got in touch with my anger. I got in touch with anger that I had stored up for decades. As a child I had never learned how to deal directly with conflict or anger. Nice people weren't supposed to get angry; we were above that; we could control our negative feelings. And control them we did, and I certainly did. I achieved surface harmony in my early relationships at the cost of emotional honesty. I never had a decent, much less an indecent, adolescent rebellion! As the elder son I took the family mantle, accepted the expectations laid upon me, particularly by my father, and sought to be a success as a Christian and as a minister.

For the last nine years I have been dealing with my anger toward my father. He has been the most powerful presence in my life: as father, as professional role model (he is a retired Bishop in the United Methodist Church), and as image of father-God. I remember watching home movies of my father and his father, observing the adulation my father gave to his father. I remember the admiration and love with which my father spoke of my grandfather over the years. I note also that my father spoke little of his mother. All the family hopes came to rest on my father. His brother Jean died of appendicitis at eighteen; his sister Rose died at birth; his sister Ruth was retarded. My father proudly told me that his father and mother joined him and my mother on their honeymoon trip west. So close were the family ties and expectations that were to affect and shape our family life down the years. For the first forty years of my life I obeyed the prescription given to me: "Get good grades, work hard, be a leader, succeed, God helps those who help themselves." No rebellion. I was the son who stayed home. The son who would have to leave home in middle age—leave the prescriptions, sort out what was real for me, own it, discard the rest, not without sorrow, and move on into my own authentic human journey. All the anger that developed in me toward my father over those decades came blasting out at Bethel. I had never established adequate distance between myself and my father, and now I needed to. I needed to withdraw from him and my mother, share less of my personal struggles with them, gather myself into a new privacy—this was hard for them to understand. My parents felt rejected, and indeed *were* being rejected, for a time, or from a time-laden way of relating, while I fought my way out of the straitjacket of my life structure into a set of clothes that fit more easily and felt more comfortable.

I got in touch with my anger toward my wife Peg. Like my father, I was paternal in my relationships with people, including my wife. I felt responsible for her happiness. She shared my dream; she was the carrier of my hopes and the supporter of my plans. Her dependence matched my paternal mode. A behavior pattern developed that seemed to meet both our needs for many years. But during those years unhealthy emotional baggage piled up for each of us. I felt that I had to contain my anger so as not to upset her. I had to learn to cope without letting my blood, sweat, and tears show. So I bottled up my anger, and in the process I unwittingly began to lose a certain kind of respect for one who, as I wrongly supposed, needed me to contain my anger for fear she wouldn't be able to handle its expression. She had to smother her own dreams, agendas, and self-development in order to be available for my agendas, to support my dreams. She had to surrender the definition of her roles and values to me, or felt she had to. We weren't aware of the anger building in each of us and were afraid of anything that might upset our "stable/productive" life. It seemed safer to maintain that paternal-dependent relationship which appeared to work so well. But underneath the "safety" of our relationship, energies were gathering which would not long be denied or caged.

When I returned from the Bethel experience, Peg and I had our frankest talk ever. I told her how I really felt about her dependence and my need to express my anger directly and honestly. She decided to go to an NTL experience herself. Ten days later we took money out of savings and she went to a week-long event near Kansas City. There she got in touch with her own anger, bottled up over the years: anger at me for my paternalism, my self-righteous containment of anger, and my refusal to acknowledge my needs and vulnerability; and anger at herself for buying into a dependent behavior pattern. She returned with those feelings churned up and raw. And for the next several years we both worked on our own angry feelings. It was a lot to work on individually, much less to be doing at the same time. It was the beginning of the end for us as a couple, an end that although wrenching and sad proved to be a healthy new beginning for each of us on our own way.

I got in touch with my anger toward the church and the ministry. I had always been a maverick in the ministry. Early I lost respect for some of what I saw in the hierarchy and the bureaucratic organization of the church and wanted to be left alone to cultivate my own parish garden.

Apprehended / 9

I expressed some of my anger by resisting or ignoring the constraints and expectations of the denominational system. I literally lost myself in my ministry, out night after night, every weekend engaged. My identity was in my vocation. If you had scratched my back a few years ago, I might have bled clergyman! I learned to live from the outside and exteriorized my feelings until they could become productive.

Sometimes I felt uncomfortable in my role as minister, and occasionally in secular company I felt ashamed or embarrassed. An important part of me—my earthiness, my meanness, my negativities—couldn't find honest expression. I was in a nice guy profession, and I discovered that I wasn't as nice a guy as I or as others had thought. I had anger and sometimes I wanted to hurt or damage other people. I discovered that there was an s.o.b. in me. What does one do in the ministry when one discovers one is something of an s.o.b.? S.o.b.'s aren't supposed to go into the ministry (although I have met a few in my time!). S.o.b.'s are supposed to become successful in politics, business, medicine, or law; these are professions in which it's okay to look out for number one.

I had emphasized in my experience and practice of Christianity a piety that was desiccated, prudish, desexed, moralistic, and legalistic. I put a smooth patina over what was rough, abrasive, ugly, and raw in me. I exalted order and tried to excommunicate chaos from myself and the systems in which I operated. In Freudian terms, I tried banishing the id, idolized the superego, and hunkered down into my ego. Bruno Bettelheim in his book *The Uses of Enchantment* gave me another view of my dilemma. In his description of the fairy tale "Sindbad the Seaman and Sindbad the Porter," he pointed out that the title suggests "the story is about the opposite aspects of one and the same person: that which pushes him to escape into a far away world of adventure and fantasy, and the other part which keeps him bound to common practicality—his id and his ego. . . ." (Biblically, one thinks of the prodigal and elder sons, and Mary and Martha as also comprehensible as different aspects of the same person.) Sindbad the Porter is the responsible, practical, duty-oriented side of the self. Sindbad the Seaman is the pleasure-oriented, venturesome, outrageous aspect of the self. The point of the story is that these two very different persons are actually brothers under the skin. "One of the great merits of this tale is that Sindbad the Seaman and Sindbad the Porter are equally appealing figures; neither of the two sides of our nature is denied its attractiveness, importance, validity."[2]

What is necessary, of course, is to deny neither aspect of the self but to seek an integration of the two parts of the self. I did not understand my need to acknowledge the s.o.b. in me, my Sindbad the Seaman. I had been trying to banish him, but he would not stay banished.

From Bethel on, I felt increasingly uneasy in my role as a parish clergyman. I had often felt that I was swimming upstream in my congregations, especially regarding social issues. I was often in the minority, whether it was civil rights, Vietnam, prison reform, tax reform, or whatever. I was fighting for change. My role as a parish clergyman meant that I had to fight with one hand behind my back, or I felt I had to. I didn't want to upset the congregation, much less split it. So I had to try to contain my passion

[2] Bruno Bettelheim, *The Uses of Enchantment* (New York: Knopf, 1977), pp. 83–86.

and make it hearable, somehow palatable. I didn't always succeed. Sometimes anger throbbed in my preaching. A woman said to me one Sunday in the 1960s, "I feel as though I have been whipped after hearing you preach." Undoubtedly I was taking out some of my inner, personal anger on these external causes and projecting my anger on others and on systems of oppression. In any case, my newly stirring anger jostled me loose from my roles. My burgeoning humanity threatened the style of my ministry. My insides were getting unruly and required my outside roles and relationships to accept a great deal more negative energy.

I got in touch with my anger toward myself. Finally, who was responsible for containing this anger all these years? I was. I had been colluding with my father, my wife, and the church to hide my negative feelings—chiefly from myself—in order to be productive in the ministry. I didn't like certain things I was discovering about myself and my roles and relationships. I no longer wanted primarily to please other people but to be *honest* with other people and myself. I wanted to be real. I wanted what was going on inside me somehow to be able to get out and express its power appropriately at home and at work. I was like that man who had been "in-valid" for thirty-eight years (John 5:2–9). I had been blaming other people and circumstances for my not being able to grasp my life and pick it up and go with it; I was letting the chips fall where they would. Questions gnawed at my insides: Do you want to be healed? Do you want to let your anger live, let it ground your warm feelings, let it break the phoniness of your nice guy smile and manner? Are you willing to risk what your anger might upset or destroy? Are you willing to let your old self be broken, disassembled, and allow time for new parts of yourself to come to light and life and find integration toward a new self?

I got in touch with my grief. "Big boys don't cry." "Bear your own burden." Other people have needs, and your ministry is to meet their needs. You are not supposed to have needs. You are supposed to be strong enough in faith to go it alone with your chin up, your head held high. My outrush of tears carried the power of decades of tears unshed, sorrow unacknowledged, defeats unadmitted, failures hidden, frustrations blocked. I *couldn't* be sad. I was a Christian! Faithful (successful?) Christians are joyous, triumphant, always overcoming evil with good, and so forth. Other people could be sad, and my job was to weep with those who weep, but to weep *their* sorrow, to wipe away *their* tears. I was not supposed to have sorrow myself or need others to put their arms around me, or go to pieces myself, or allow myself to descend into despair. I was supposed to be consistently positive and cheerful. So I learned to make that happen, burying my sorrow beneath my sincere smiles.

Only now my grief powered through all my defenses, like water bursting through a dam. The tributaries of thousands of little defeats, failures, and losses trickled down through the decades into one raging river of tears. I grieved my lost adolescence I never had, never allowed myself. I grieved for all the far countries I never wandered into. I grieved for the prodigal son in me that had never lived. I grieved for my repressed Zorba. (It wasn't coincidence that I was forty-four years old when the dam broke. Adult development theory suggests that it is in the middle years when one becomes aware of one's own death, of the fact that one doesn't have forever. One sees both horizons now: sunrise, sunset. Aging parents, departing children, ceilings on the career, struggles in marriage, and a wounded/straitjacketed self all clamor to be heard.) I am vulnerable. I do hurt. I am disappointed. I am afraid. I want someone to put his arms around me. I need to cry my own tears. I am ready to walk my own shadowed valleys. The soil of my self-system got plowed and the ferment of my grief abounded, and for the next several years I learned more about anguish than I had known was in me. I began to be broken.

I got in touch with my sexual energy. I had such virginity rules drummed into me in my boyhood that you wouldn't believe it. Or, maybe you would. I obeyed them. I took to myself a narrow concept of purity and tried to live it, and in the living of it, purity became prudery and prurience. I remember during the civil rights riots of the 1960s in Philadelphia, where I was co-minister of the First United Methodist Church of Germantown, my feeling of offense at the obscenities the Philadelphia police shouted as they chased and beat black youths. The four-letter words in me were locked up, and the expression of them by others was doubly offensive, resonating as they did to unexpressed rage within me.

I baffled and muffled my sexuality. I sublimated its power to productive results for my ministry. There was a period in my late thirties when I went to a doctor to inquire about my low sexual drive. What was the matter? It wasn't impotence, although an experience with that came later. It was low interest. Peg and I were both worried. The doctor assured me that it was all in my head. And that, in fact, is where it was, unconnected with my deepest insides, building, building there in the dark. And so it began to leak out in sneaky, smirky little ways, little bits of flirting that never led to anything, never amounted to anything, but left me feeling dirty and blocked. For all those decades my Puritan defenses were adequate to hold back the pounding energies. But at Bethel the dam broke and all those longings and yearnings poured out. The power that had not found healthy experimentation in adolescence or uninhibited expression as a young adult now had to be dealt with at midlife. The fences were going down, and the orderly structure that had been so productive for so long was cracking. As I struggled to express all the strange new energies and still keep it all together, I came to know that I couldn't do it.

The logjam was breaking. I couldn't guarantee everything. I couldn't control it all anymore, maybe not even manage it. It wasn't that I was frantic or frenetic or wild and foolish but that I was getting up after those thirty-eight "in-valid" years, and I staggered without my crutches. And I couldn't tell, didn't know, had no way of knowing where it would all go. I was scared. I might have tried to put a lock on it all. I might have opted for safety. I perhaps could have found more acceptable, more conventional ways of putting myself and my life together. But, whatever, I decided to go with the new energies, acknowledge my own needs, honor my own inner agenda, and let the winds fill the sail of my life and blow me out to sea, out of the safe harbor and haven.

The summer all this was breaking out in me was in 1973. On July 12 of that year, my forty-seventh birthday, one of my daughters and Peg got me a birthday present, a small metal sculpture of an eagle mounted on a driftwood base and launched for takeoff. The beak of the eagle is wide open as though in a great shout or cry. The wings are spread and mounting up (Isaiah 40:31). One foot is in the air, the other just touching the base. Neither they nor I realized what an apt symbol it was of where I was in my life. I was about to take off.

What happened to me, in me, that night at Bethel? I was touched to my core, my defenses were overwhelmed, I was turned inside out. A priest once said to me, "You Protestants stress comprehension, we Catholics stress apprehension." I, who had been trained to comprehend life and to manage it accordingly, now found myself apprehended by a strange power. Ambushed, like Moses; mugged, like Jacob; arrested, like Paul.

> Lovers and madmen have such seething brains
> Such shaping fantasies, that apprehend
> More than cool reason ever comprehends.
> The lunatic, the lover and the poet
> Are of imagination all compact. . . . [3]

The lunatic, the lover, and the poet came alive in me, overwhelming cool reason, to my delight and terror. Spirit was searching my innermost heart with sighs too deep for words, erupting in my anger, grief, and sexual energy— those primary energies that power our being and doing more fundamentally than doctrines and designs. An initiative was taken with me. Chaotic energy broke apart my fragile order and left me shivering.

Everything in my life went up for grabs at Bethel, including part of my belief system. How did my intentions and hopes connect with God's will for me? I returned to my biblical roots, seeking meaning in the narratives and exploits of those ancient wanderers and journey-makers. I saw myself here and there, and especially came home in the story of Abraham and Sarah. Their story is mine and

---

[3] William Shakespeare, *A Midsummer Night's Dream,* act V, scene 1.

mine theirs. It is the story of people uprooted well along in their lives, people who choose to leave the security of home to go on a wilderness journey to seek a new homeland. In the years that followed Bethel, I struggled to understand myself on the journey I chose and for which I was chosen.

> By faith Abraham obeyed when he was called to go out to a place which he was to receive as an inheritance. . . .
>
> *Hebrews 11:8a*

What does it mean to be called? Even though many people have mystical experiences in the course of their lives, such experiences may not result in a decision to leave one's old life and strike out for the new. More of us experience that sudden imperative in our bottom line needs and wants, fears and hopes pressing to the surface of decision. A call may come as a nudge, glimpse, touch, glance, fresh insight, or tearing sorrow. It may come in the earthquake of anger, grief, sexual energy, or in a still small voice. However it comes, the initiative of an alien/friendly power strikes us with surprise and disruption. I was taken by the scruff of my life and shaken loose from the securities and identities that had served me, or that I had served, for forty-four years. I was mugged in the night by a strange inner assailant.

There is the story of a Jew who wanted to go to Ireland all his life; he saved up his money and finally got a two-week vacation in Belfast. He'd heard about the religious problem there, but was sure that it would not touch him. The first night there he left his hotel, took a walk, and as he was coming back to the hotel was mugged on the street. His mugger whispered hoarsely to him, "What religion are you?" He thought to himself, "Oh, thank

God," and said, "I'm Jewish." Whereupon his mugger said, "I must be the luckiest Arab in all Belfast."

Where we think we're invulnerable, we may in fact be most vulnerable to that teasing/overshadowing Spirit apprehending us on our blind side, that Spirit falling upon us, overtaking us, undermining us, overwhelming us.

What does it mean to be "called?" Jung's language helps me here. He said, "Trust your own meaning, follow your own meaning, let it guide you." If "call" is an external term, "meaning" is an internal term. To be called means no longer to locate our deepest authority in a book or commandment or system or any external place at all but in the depths of our own existence. It means to listen for leading in our own sighs and songs. Paul Tillich once said to a friend, "Follow your own eros." If we follow our own eros/meaning/yearning, we may get in touch with the energy of our destiny. Praying is trusting that inner movement of meaning and yielding to its imperatives.

I felt called out of yesterday toward tomorrow, out of grave clothes into nakedness, vulnerability, possibility. Something deeper than right and wrong was happening. The particularity of right and wrong choices is important, but our choices are interladen with good and bad outcomes for ourselves and other people, and there can be no neat assessment of where truth might be. Sometimes the inner compulsion is great enough to power us through mixed moral situations. So it was for me. There is a Lutheran "trust God and sin on boldly" character to our deepest life movements. We simply can't tell and don't know, and no one else can tell us, although some will try, what is our authentic calling to move out. We have to risk, leap, leave ... or stay. We wonder: Is doing my thing doing the right thing? Is denying my thing doing the right thing? Who knows ahead of time? Nobody. Even the Son doesn't know (Mark 13: 32). Faith is not knowledge.

What does it mean to obey our calling? Obey is a word and concept I rebel against. My rule-oriented background has caused me to need to break laws and exceed limits just to be able to establish my own identity and integrity. Obedience smacks of submission, which is different from trust, and does not seem to require me to be adult and take authority and responsibility for my own life. If I am to be responsible for my own life, I must have authority to make my own decisions. If obedience meant staying put and being "a good boy" and doing what others expected of me, then I was no longer prepared to do that. God's will played in my head as a parent tape, a shaking finger, a disapproving frown, a "no." I would disobey that external will if that's what it took to honor the deepest movement of my spirit. Yet I didn't believe, couldn't believe, that in honoring the deepest integrity of my being and moving with it I was fundamentally going counter to right and truth. But I couldn't connect; I couldn't make sense of what I knew I had to do. The faith system that had served me so well, or which I had served so well for so many years, was no longer adequate to guide me. In a new and dark way I was on my own.

But, what if obeying our calling means to respond to the new energies churning out of our deepest integrity? Obeying our calling might mean having the courage, as did Abraham and Sarah, to obey that inner yearning calling us to leave home and go out on a wilderness journey. It might mean being obedient toward our own meaning and responsible toward our own destiny. Being called might mean being found, discovering that we belong to the world, that we have enough worth to be invited, urged, and summoned to participate in a work in the world. It might mean realizing, with a fierce joy, that tomorrow's truth beckons us in our wants as well as in our oughts, as often in those inner agendas that swell within us as in those outer agendas put upon us by peers, parents, colleagues, and constituents. Obeying our calling, following Jesus, might mean not imitating him in the sense of seeking to become a carbon copy of him, but like him, living out of our deepest integrity in response to God and neighbor. It might mean looking for tomorrow's signals in our needs as well as our duties, knowing that God exults when one comes through with a wish of one's own. While taking the markings along the trail—those outer agendas of church and world—seriously, obeying the Spirit might mean honoring those sighs too deep for words in the depths of our own being in the confidence that we are being drawn, propelled, called, nudged, and wooed by a lover . . . one who calls us out of our time and place toward a new time and place. We are in the hands of one who loves us. Obedience has nothing to do with punishment but with promise, nothing to do with submission but with responsibility, nothing to do with compromise but with choice, nothing to do with being right but with being real. "Not my will but thine be done" is not a call to self-destruction but to self-giving. Christ does not seek our death that he might live in us, but he seeks to live in us that we might be reborn. When we are called, our obedience is our honest response to the movements of Spirit in us and beyond us. What we have to do is respond. Later will be time enough to try to untangle the threads of our histories to discern what was right and wrong, creative and destructive. We cannot know ahead of time. We can count on forgiveness, not as cheap grace, but as the costly grace of one who, before us, left family, synagogue, and tradition to move to the edges of his own estate.

The ways we obey our calling will reflect our own individuality and style. At one time the chairman of the board of a church I then served said to me, "Bob, if we needed three yards for a first down over center, I would give you the ball every time. But if we needed to run around end or throw a screen pass, someone else would have to do it." He was commenting on my driving, straight-ahead, unsubtle, and insensitive style of leadership, my "make it happen" approach to life, my inability to "let it happen," to be subtle, supple, sensitive. That's the way I obeyed my call, with a go-for-broke plunge through the center of my life and context.

Let me now raise a cautionary note. There is a critical difference between being apprehended, always a mysterious event, and being managed by some packaged group process. Any system of disciplines, ancient or modern, that can produce a predictable outcome cannot be identified with the event of being apprehended by Spirit. Spirit is as likely or as unlikely to be moving in such experiences as in any other of our daily happenings. The particular process, whether it is that of a marathon, Cursillo, est, TM, TA, Ignation exercises, or whatever, cannot guarantee the presence of Spirit. Indeed, the more tailored, unvariable, and predictable the process and the result, the more wary we should be of claims that God is involved in it. Both human potential gurus and old-time religious revivalists have found effective ways of breaking down the defenses of people in a given context and opening them up. What the people are opened up to is a welter of creative and destructive energies that have been blocked. A process may be gentle or coercive. A gentle process, a process of calling Lazarus to come out of his tomb, and letting him out on his own time and at his own pace, is more likely to be a process in which Spirit is moving than a coercive one. Lazarus needs to be carefully unwrapped. And yet it is also true that sometimes a raging wind may strip us of bandages and old clothes that are no longer appropriate for us, and Spirit may be in that raging storm of tears, anger, sexual energy, and yearnings for intimacy and hope. Those who work with groups should remember that there is the tendency to brainwash participants in everyone's process, overtly or covertly, "because it is good for them." Discerning whether the Spirit is in a given process or place is both an ongoing task and gift.

I admit to a quandary here. At Kirkridge, the retreat and study center that I direct in northeastern Pennsylvania, we have finely honed the process of our Midlife Journey Workshop. We arrange and expedite a carefully orchestrated event with various components that, we have learned over a period of time, enable people to come to grips with their own midlife tasks. It is tempting to think that we have arranged the conditions in which Spirit will apprehend people. But we haven't. Nobody can do that. Spirit appears to be more interested in everyday happenings as a context for movement than in elitist, packaged, or severely ascetic systems of spiritual growth. I have a Jeffersonian rather than a Hamiltonian view of the operation of Spirit. I am fundamentally skeptical of all systems (religious or secular) that guarantee rebirth; transformation; new life; the new you in three days, one month, or three years. Part of my wariness may have to do with my disinterest in or unwillingness to adhere to such systems for very long. My life seems to overwhelm all my careful rationalizations and tidy orderliness. But more deeply, I think that highly intentional seeking after spiritual development is ambiguous because it can insulate us from compassion and may turn privacy into privatism. We are reminded that those who hunger and thirst for justice are blessed (Matthew 5:6), not necessarily those who hunger and thirst for spiritual growth. It is possible to have an inordinate preoccupation with our own spiritual development, just as it is possible to be indifferent to it altogether. And Spirit, as we have seen, takes us by surprise in the mystery of its own initiatives. So we should design our disciplines and impose them with knowledge of their limits and our fallibility.

Abraham and Sarah obeyed a call to go and receive an inheritance. It is important not to miss the inheritance. One is foolish to set out on a risky journey . . . for nothing. But Abraham and Sarah had a promise, a gift of a new time and place. What we may inherit is surely nothing we could have earned, achieved, deserved, or produced. It is something appealing, valuable, promising, exciting, hopeful—or we wouldn't jeopardize all we are and have to go in search of it. We give an inheritance only to someone we love and trust. Inheritance is given out of love, and so it must be good, although it may also be costly and painful to own. Our inheritance has our name on it. Hidden in it is the gift of our identity, our new name, and our new vocation. Our inheritance might mean a new relationship with ourselves, our spouses, our parents, and our children. It might mean a new ministry, a new vocation. Spirit is at work a generation before the crisis emerges in the culture, and years before the crisis emerges in the person. When there is that disruptive call, then we can take it as prima facie evidence that life has not abandoned us, that we are valuable, that we are worth the anguish of rebirth. To be in the hands of the living God is a fearful and a hopeful thing. To be apprehended is to find out that no external power has pulled a string, but that an inner trap door has been released. We find ourselves falling out of yesterday's securities and constraints toward tomorrow's movements and meanings. Calling is falling. Obeying is going out not knowing. Being apprehended means leaving home.

Where are you taking me? Will I be safe? What will happen to those I love? Everything is falling. I'm scared. Don't shake me to pieces. Don't destroy me. Leave me a place to stand or sit or kneel or lie down. The waters are going over me. I can't see the way ahead. Lord, be gentle with me, let your wind die down a little. Let your fire warm me, but don't burn all my house down.

2 | Leaving Home

By faith Abraham obeyed when he was called to go
out to a place which he was to receive as an
inheritance, and he went out, not knowing where he
was to go.

Hebrews 11:8

ABRAHAM and Sarah left home. We can imagine their friends and relatives saying to them in a hundred ways: "Don't leave home! Enjoy! You've worked hard and done well. You're home safe. Don't throw it all away for a wild dream. You don't know what you're getting into. Things will never again be the same." But Abraham and Sarah left home—late in life. And things never were the same again. They didn't know what they were getting into. But they knew they had to leave. The time had come to leave, to say goodby to life as it had always been. They couldn't really explain it to others, but something inside them would not be denied, could not be ignored, had to be honored, no matter who understood or didn't. Abraham and Sarah left home.

I left home the day after Christmas 1973. I had been married for twenty-three years, most of them happy and productive years. Since Bethel, Peg and I had been struggling, each separately with our own jumble of identities and feelings and together with the behavior pattern that had become destructive and unfulfilling for us both. I knew I had to leave. I who had it made professionally, who for the first time in my life was developing some financial security, who loved my family and delighted in summer family gatherings at my parents' cottage in Michigan, who liked the power that was in my hands, who had always managed well and succeeded in conventional terms. I knew I had to leave home and put it all to risk. So the day after Christmas I left home.

A friend, whose car was large enough to pull a small U-Haul trailer, helped me load my books and a few pieces of furniture onto the trailer. I was moving to an apartment. I watched his car pull the U-Haul out of the driveway of my family house. A U-Haul. My life reduced to some books and a few sticks of furniture on a moving U-Haul wagon. My U-Haul life. I noticed the words painted on the rear of the departing wagon: *Adventure in Moving. U-Haul It. Rent One Way. Anywhere.* I was moving out of the house where my children lived, moving away from them, never again to live with them in the daily life of resident parent and children. Yes, I would have to haul my own life. I would be renting an apartment. The divorce process wiped out my modest financial assets. No longer would I be an owner, but a renter. *One way.* One way. It *felt* and it *was* so final, so irrevocable. No return ticket this time. No way back to the way things used to be. "The way we were" was over. The end of the good old days. What would the new days be like? One way . . . *anywhere.* No specific destination. No certain place to go to. No new home in sight. A temporary apartment, a journey, a time of leaving home.

Faith involves leaving home. Obeying a fresh call of God means leaving home. Leaving our provisional homes, roles, relationships, lands, belief systems, life styles—all, to go out in search of an abiding homeland. Don't misunderstand me. Abraham and Sarah left home *together.* For most people leaving home in response to a fresh call from God does not mean getting separated and divorced, leaving one's job and house, although it did mean those things for me. Leaving home as a faithful response is for everybody. The particularities of our calling and our leaving vary as richly and diversely as do our lives. Leaving home means leaving imperatives and agendas that are no longer healthy, fulfilling, fitting. Leaving home means moving out into a transitional period, which is characterized by renting rather than owning, one way rather than round trip, anywhere rather than a known somewhere. It is frightening, scary, risky, promising, and energizing. Jesus said to his disciples on one occasion, "If any one comes to me and does not hate his own father and mother and wife and children and brothers and sisters, yes, and even his own life, he cannot be my disciple" (Luke 14:26). Jesus then told a story about counting the costs before one risks his life in the venture of discipleship. We might say at this point that it also takes courage to stay home and continue the struggle there. Leaving home can mean letting go of old patterns of behavior and perception and moving into new patterns, in the same roles, relationships, and places.

A faithful leaving home means saying "no" to yesterday's will of God, which is now a still photo, to be free to say "yes" to today's will of God, which is an unprecedented moving picture. No one can tell you or me what today's will of God is for us. We have to decide for ourselves. We have no advance guarantees, no blessed assurances, no certainties. We have to decide in faith and go out not knowing. The nets and structures of our lives are always provisional.

It is painful to leave home. Leaving is grieving, for our losses are real and there is tragedy in our lives as well as transformation. There is death as well as rebirth. Indeed, unless there is death there can be no rebirth. Rebirth comes only out of what is dying. We musn't dote on the past, because doting distorts the present, but grieving allows the past to be gathered, celebrated, offered, and released. Grieving allows the future to be born in us and those new yearnings to live and shape our tomorrows.

For me, leaving home meant leaving Peg after twenty-three years. How could we do it? How could I do it? During the months of deciding, a recurring image flashed across my mind. Peg and I were in a deer park; I was the warden, and she was the helpless and defenseless deer. I, the warden, whose job it was to protect the deer from harm, to take care of it, instead turned and shot the deer between the eyes. Later, as I described this image to a counselor, he suggested I revise the image so that instead of shooting the deer between the eyes, I see myself as the warden opening the gate of the park so that the deer would now be free to go out and find her own life, free of being fenced in and confined by me, the warden. (Years later, Peg told me that is exactly what had happened.) But I experienced considerable guilt in my own decision making. It took a deep and constant inner knowledge of what I must do to keep me going. Our fields of energy were not complementary or mutually facilitative but destructive and deadening. I needed in the woman near me quietness, self-containment, understatement, and clear boundaries. I needed to be able to express my anger directly without fear of destroying or being destroyed. She needed to let her assertive energies pour out in the redefining of her identity and vocation. The fit between our diverging needs and journeys was bad.

William Gibson's play *A Cry of Players*[1] is about the young William Shakespeare. He loves his young wife Anne and his baby daughter Susanna. But he also loves the plays that the traveling companies bring to his little town. Those companies leave his little town, and he longs to go with them. His own vocation is calling him. He has a terrible decision: to stay with his wife and child and lose his vocation, his self, or to leave with the traveling players, without his wife and daughter, with no guarantee as to when they will be together again, if ever. There is a heart-rending scene as the young Will says to the departing players:

WILL [*Shouts*]: I'm coming!

· · · ·

ANNE: Them, ye're going with—
WILL: Yes.
ANNE: —them, now? But none of us—Lad, we can't—
WILL: Alone.
ANNE: Alone!

· · · ·

WILL: I can't live with you. Not now, not—live—

· · · ·

ANNE: Ye're—leaving me, lad? Ye won't—send for us—
WILL: If I can.
ANNE: —or ever come back—
WILL [*Desperate*]: If I can! Not now. . . . If I keep you now I lose myself. Don't you see?
        (*She sees, bows to it, yes.*)
        Make me that gift—
ANNE: No.

---

[1] William Gibson, *A Cry of Players* (New York: Atheneum, 1969), pp. 152–55 (selected).

WILL: —of myself. Let me go. (*A whisper.*) Let me go—
ANNE: No—
  (*But at last she releases his wrist; he snatches up the sack, and backs away.*)
WILL: God forgive me.
  (*He turns, and runs stumbling off. Anne bends over Susanna's head. . . .*)

For me, leaving home meant leaving my parents, especially my father. Leaving in the sense of making decisions and moves in my life that were bound to be displeasing and unsettling to my parents. I had never disestablished myself from my father in my teens. As the eldest son I took the family mantle and went to a theological seminary, as did my two brothers. I accepted my father's agenda for his life as my agenda for my life. I was the dutiful son who set about fulfilling the expectations of his parents. I no longer blame my parents nor myself for being such a son. I chose the path they wanted me to choose. I went out knowing where I was to go.

So, inevitably, over the years the anger built up in me as my own inner agenda began to gather. I had been theologically imprisoned in the concept that God wanted me to take care of others' needs and submerge my own needs, sublimating them and transmuting them into productive energy for others. The concept held in my mind longer than it did in my heart. I finally came to understand that it was okay to honor my own needs as well as those of others. I came to understand that it was now time for me, the eldest son, to leave home. [We remember in Jesus' story of the prodigal and elder sons (Luke 15:11–32) that only by leaving home and coming to terms with himself could the younger son eventually return to his father for the reunion of adult and adult. The elder son who never left home never could be at home with himself or with his father.]

In the Autumn of 1973 I went to tell my parents that I was soon leaving Peg and First Community Church, my congregation in Columbus, Ohio, and didn't know what lay ahead. They were upset. I stayed with them a few days. One day my father and I were sitting on a bench. He turned to me and said, "You are the shepherd of the sheep. You have become a wolf that has ravaged the flock." Those words went like a spear into my heart. Part of my insides said, "You're right, Dad!" Another part of me said, "Bullshit, Dad!" I had displeased my father in the process of holding to my own integrity. I did not then know whether I was also displeasing my father God. I feared perhaps I was, yet I knew deep down that I had to do what I was doing, and I trusted that God was with me, at least in forgiveness and understanding, and maybe even strengthening me with the courage to go out not knowing, and to risk all that was most precious to me in family and ministry for a promise, a yearning, a direction, a hope. As I reflect now on my father's comment, I realize that the shepherd in me—the gentle, paternal, protective, nurturing part of me—had predominated in my life and ministry. It was now time for the "wolf" in me, the violent energy, the savage anger, the raw power, to be acknowledged, accepted, and integrated into a fresh self-system. The truth is that each of us is both violent and gentle and has the capacity both to create and destroy. It is interesting that more than one pacifist is a deeply violent human being, whose external ideology constrains violent energies within. For me, at least, the wolf needed to be acknowledged, toward that day when in psychological and theological terms the wolf and the sheep, the lion and the lamb would lie down together in me in wholeness and integrity of being.

I entered into a period of several years of struggle with my father in which each of us, now standing on separate turf, sought to understand himself and the other in new terms. The Bishop, and the son of a Bishop! At one time I thought we could work it out to a neat and tidy closure, set it all up on a shelf, and let it be. And indeed, we have worked it through to a point where the tension is gentle and the affection and respect we feel for each other prevail. Yet, the full understanding is still missing. And I realize it may always be that way. To say hello to myself, I had to say goodby to my father. As I try to hear my children say goodby to me, I want to understand that it is the only way they can say hello to their own lives. But it is still difficult. "Love is not to be paid back, it is to be passed on."[2] Yes, we know that, but it is still difficult. We want our children to pay us back by living a life style and value system of which we approve. Why don't they listen to our wisely drawn designs for their lives? Why do they insist on choosing their own partners, vocations, life patterns? Because they have to leave home to arrive on the threshold of their own journeys. So I am still leaving my parents, although I come home to them often in letters, and visits, and prayers, and phone calls. And it bothers me less than it used to that there may never be understanding of the whys of my choices. We can fully love one another without fully understanding one another.

---

[2] Herbert Tarr, *The Conversion of Chaplain Cohen* (New York: Geis, 1963). [This book is out of print, but a section in which this quote appears is in Robert Raines, *Creative Brooding* (New York: Macmillan, 1966).]

For me, leaving home meant leaving my children, even as
they were leaving me. Usually, in one's middle age one's
children are leaving home themselves. Two of mine were
already on their way, and another was soon to go. So the
time of the breakup of the family unit was upon us in any
case. Yet I left my children to become a commuter father, a
corresponding father. I discovered that whereas I used to
relate to "my children," "the family" in toto, now there
was no longer "the family" as it had been. And in fact I
now had four distinct relationships with four different
offspring. Each relationship needed to be experienced,
fostered, and developed in particular ways.

The most painful part of leaving my children was the
loss of the delight of daily living with my then eight-year-
old son Bob. My girls were on their way. But my one son
was home. And I was leaving home. I was leaving him at
home. I cried about him and over him often in those first
months away from him. I cried for myself. I cried for us
both. And I set about doing those things that would help
him and me develop our father-son communion together
even when separated by 400 miles. I urged him to do what
my father had urged me to do when I went away into the
service and then to college: to write a letter a week, or at
least very often. And he pretty well obeyed me, as I had
obeyed my father. And so we wrote each other. His letters
would typically end with a huge "Love, Bob." I addressed
his letters "Robert Arnold Raines, Junior," claiming and
naming him as my son, as unique to me as a boy in all the
world. We knew we had something special together.

Bob is hyper with energy. In the daytime when we're
on vacation together, he is consumed with playing ball,
swimming, ping-pong, nonstop talking ("Rest your mouth,

Bob," one of his sisters would say to him). But at night, going to bed, while I was rubbing his back, the times of quiet self-revelation would come upon us. I learned early to listen and wait. In the autumn of 1975 he made All Stars in his Little League football. It meant a lot to him, sports nut that he was and is. I visited him in Peg's home where he lived. As I was putting him to bed that night, out of the quiet he said to me, "Dad, is this the first time you ever rubbed an All Star's back?" I grinned to myself in the darkness, felt a lump rising in my throat, and mustered presence of mind to say, "Yes, I guess it is." He was feeling like an All Star in his father's hands, and I was feeling the love of a father hearing the heart of his son. Everyone needs to feel that he or she is an All Star sometime, somewhere, with someone, not for *doing* well at football or anything else, but just for *being* who he or she is.

One night at my home in Pennsylvania I was putting Bob to bed. It was the winter of 1977. A friend and colleague of mine was at the house; we were leading a retreat together on the theme: A Fresh Look at the Communion of the Saints. We had been laughing, talking, and joking together, and Bob had overheard us and enjoyed our laughter. He asked me what the Communion of the Saints was about, and I told him it had to do with what people hoped for. Out of the quiet he asked me, "What do you hope for, Dad?" I received his question and pondered it and began to tell him I hoped for peace in my life and in the world, for healthy opportunities for him and all children to develop and grow, for his sisters, his mother, and for myself. And then I asked him, "What do you hope for, Bob?" And he said to me, "I have everything I want, Dad, except that sometimes I wish you and Mom still lived together."

The pain of not living with Bob has eased. He is healthy and happy. We love each other. We enjoy writing, talking on the phone, and especially the times we are together. I learned to put my own pain in perspective. In Paul Cowan's review of Gerald Stern's book *The Buffalo Creek Disaster*, I came upon this passage.

> In one vignette, he [Stern] describes Roland Staten, a miner who managed to jump off his house when it was carried away by rushing waters, holding onto his son. His 5½-month pregnant wife was trapped. . . . Staten recalled, "When I looked back and saw her, she said, 'Take care of my baby.' . . . That's the last time I saw her." Now he must live with the unrelenting, guilt-provoking knowledge that he couldn't even fulfill that request. Moments later, he said, he was still hanging onto the boy but the water was rushing so fast, "I was thrown from side to side and crushed—my insides was crushed so hard that it just seemed my eyeballs was trying to pop out, and my breath, I couldn't get my breath at all. Somewhere along there I lost that boy of mine. I don't know where. By that time he had stopped screaming and drunk so much water and everything—I don't know what happened to him."[3]

I am grateful for life. I accept the small pain of geographical separation.

For me, leaving home meant leaving my role as a parish minister. I had served three parishes over a period of twenty years. I learned to do it well, on the whole, and I enjoyed it, on the whole. But discontent and confinement began to grow in me. Sometimes I wondered what I would have been like in another profession or if I had developed

---

[3] Paul Cowan, "The Buffalo Creek Disaster," *The New York Times Book Review*, Sept. 5, 1976, pp. 6, 7.

my own business. Sometimes I fantasized about being thrown out on the street, having to get up and start from scratch in something, and seeing what I could make of myself. Something in me wanted to risk again vocationally. And something in me wanted something more out of me. Undeveloped parts of myself yearned for attention. I was ready to try something, but I didn't know what, and it was scary. I knew how to be a parish minister. I didn't know what else I might learn to do. Who would pay me to do what *I* wanted to do? When I decided to move toward a divorce, I knew that I would have to leave my parish soon.

In fact, I resigned in February of 1974, two months after moving out of my home. I had some ideas about doing a study on midlife, but beyond that I did not know what I would do or where I would go. But I was leaving the parish ministry after twenty years of practice. Perhaps I would return to it at sometime in the future, perhaps not. But one thing was clear, I was leaving it now. My ministry was not concluded, but my ministry in the parish was ending, for a time. My developing self had pressed against the contours and confines of my role for some time. I was feeling the need for privacy, a privacy that was difficult to attain as a parish clergyman. Wherever I went in my town, I was the minister. Something clicked in people's heads when they saw me. In my own head, I was switched on "minister" most of the time. For many years my self-understanding was totally into that role. Who was I? I was a minister. But I was more than, and less than, and other than, a clergyman even as I *was* a clergyman. The role of parish minister began to suit the self emerging in me less and less authentically. I knew that deciding to leave my home also meant that I must leave this parish and this role, going out not knowing where I was to go. I felt I was not abdicating my ministry but leaving a particular expression of it. More fundamentally, I was establishing some needed distance between myself and my role and discovering an identity that could include a clergy role but was not defined, exhausted, or expressed totally in it.

In Leonard Bernstein's *Mass*, the celebrant who is Every Man has robe after robe laid on him by others or by himself. Layer upon layer of expectation go over him—the constraints of custom, the straitjacket of obligation—until he literally staggers under the burden of all those investments laid on him. Finally, driven to extremity, in a wild and frightening scene he literally tears off the vestments, layer after layer, turning, twisting, ripping, stretching, until he stands clear and free before the altar, divested in the presence of the people under God. He has ripped off his own grave clothes to become vulnerable and real in the world.

For me, leaving home meant leaving a concept of God that no longer worked for me. My image of God's will for me broke. I had been raised to think of God's will as something objective out there in a book or commandment or counselor, some external authority that would identify the right and verify its imperative for my life. Something I was supposed to decipher and then do, some toting up of the pros and cons of things that would yield *the answer*. But in my searching and struggle to honor what was happening inside me, as well as to honor expectations and obligations from outside me, I couldn't make them match. They came out differently. I had to choose. All my life I had chosen, so I thought, to meet the obligations of church and society and family and parents, believing that God's will was to be found in those responsibilities. But now, something deeper than my ability to comprehend or rationalize was moving in me. I found myself moving in directions that could result in seeming to say "no" to some of the primary obligations of my life or at least to see those obligations in a different light. And where was God in it? Would such a movement mean disobeying God? I didn't know. I could find no balance sheet to yield *the answer,* no satisfying way to please God and everybody else and myself. How to sort out conflicting claims, demands, expectations, agendas, wants, needs? There was no blessed assurance in prayer or anywhere else for me. I had to make my own decisions in the dark, own them, pay the costs for them, and move on out.

In these years of deciding I went to see a friend, a Roman Catholic priest, several times to share what was happening in me and ask his judgement. One time he said to me, "Your doctrine of God's will is obsolete for you. The weight of your experience is too heavy to be carried any longer by your concept of God's will. It isn't that God's will for you is broken, but that your understanding of God's will is broken. You're going to have to live and decide for a time in the dark." I discovered that many of the answers of my theology as well as of my life were provisional, partial, limited. I discovered that I had been living mainly by knowledge instead of faith. And now, there was no alternative to living by faith. I didn't choose faith, faith chose me. God yanked me out of my theological straitjacket and left me naked for a while, naked of satisfying theological concepts. I still found comfort and meaning in the biblical stories, however. And it was there that I found myself at home even as I was leaving home. For the Bible is about journeys and pilgrims. Human journeys to God, and God's journey *to* humanity and *with* humanity and *for* humanity. I knew I was in and on that journey, and although I was uncertain in what degree I was obeying or disobeying God's will in my choices, my deepest self never doubted God's hand holding me. "If I take the wings of the morning and dwell in the uttermost parts of the sea, even there thy hand shall lead me and thy right hand shall hold me" (Psalm 139:9-10, KJV). And somewhere inside I thought, "Maybe God is cheering for me, cheering me on, calling me, pushing me out of the nest of the first half of my life, calling me to learn to fly all over again, in new ways, into the second half of my life." I began to trust that God was sometimes in my wants as well as in my oughts. It comforted and exhilarated me to recall that Jesus tuned into the wants of people. To the man in-valid for thirty-eight years he said, "Do you want to be healed?" (John 5:6). To his disciples James and John he said, "What do you want me to do for you?" (Mark 10:51). Jesus respected and directly addressed the longings and hopes of people. The positive energy hidden in our wants is the energy of transformation and rebirth. It is the energy that can create a new future. It is the energy that can pick up a broken life and walk with it toward tomorrow with courage and dignity and on its own power.

In a fundamental way I came to trust that God was for me and with me. *Indeed, the decisions that took me away from home and left me vulnerable could never have been made except on the basis of a trust in God deeper than my ability to rationalize, protect, anticipate, or justify even to myself.* What I mean is not that I trusted in God but that God trusted in me, and I believed it with my body, my life, my most precious inheritance. It isn't that we have faith in God but that God believes in us, not that we hope in God but that his hope for us remains unshaken, not that we love him but that he loves us. It is God's hold on us that is unbreakable and does not finally have to do with human distinctions between right and wrong but with the fidelity of a love which will not let us go.

For me, leaving home meant leaving a primary concern for the validation of myself by others to an acceptance of self-validation. Because I trusted in my deepest center that God affirmed me and that, therefore, I could affirm myself, I was now less dependent on the affirmation of others. I wanted to be real and whole more than I wanted to be applauded and honored. I wanted to hear one hand clapping inside me more than many hands clapping in the sanctuary. I could hear that distant drumbeat sound within, and it was time to obey it, follow it, step to it, learn its rhythm and cadence, and discover it as my authentic dance, even if it meant stepping outside the drill team lineup.

Carola Mann, a psychoanalyst and midlife researcher, has written of a movement across the midlife years from "us-ness to me-ness." A movement from primary self-identification in terms of roles and relationships to a primary self-identification in terms of one's experience of oneself. This process, which Jung calls "individuation," happens only through multiple experiences of separation and loss. It is movement into a responsible autonomy in which one takes one's signals from within and directs his life from his own center. This is not selfishness in the sense of being *self-centered* (although it can become so); it has rather to do with being *centered in the self*. It is movement into a time when one is no longer seeking permission or making apology for the choices one makes.

Levinson reminds us that at midlife the person who has been changing, growing, developing, maturing will need to take stock of the goodness or badness of fit between the self and any part of its life structure. For some people the fit will be good and a little adjustment is all that is needed. For some other people the fit in one aspect or another will be bad and radical change will need to be made. For most people the fit will be a mix of good and bad, and several years will be required to move creatively and constructively towards a more healthy congruence, coherence, integration, wholeness. The period of change, transition, passage will be a time of vulnerability, when the clear order and rigid structures of yesterday are being dismantled, and for a time the creature is without its protective as well as its restrictive shell. The soil of identity is loosened, ploughed up, and its new fruit is not yet visible much less marketable. The roots of the emerging self are still hidden. It is a good time to pray:

> May he give you the power through his Spirit for your hidden self to grow strong, so that Christ may live in your hearts through faith, and then, planted in love and built on love, you will with all the saints have strength to grasp the breadth and the length, the height and the depth, until knowing the love of Christ, which is beyond all knowledge, you are filled with the utter fullness of God.
>
> *Ephesians 3:16–19,* JB

For me, leaving home meant having to learn how to say "goodby." In his book *The Living Reminder*, Henri Nouwen suggests that we need to cultivate "the art of leaving . . . the ability to be articulately absent . . . creative withdrawal."[4] The art of leaving: to allow space for another to expand, develop, be. Nouwen reminds us that

---

[4] Henri Nouwen, *The Living Reminder* (New York: Seabury Press, 1977), p. 44.

only as we leave do others depending upon us receive the space they need to grow in their own strength. When I left home Peg had my paternal umbrella removed and was free for the first time in twenty-three years to imagine, design, and construct her own life. She took charge. Several years later, she is remarried, a Ph.D. candidate in the field of counseling, and by her own account more happy and fulfilled than ever before.

A friend of mine used to worry out loud at the time of his annual vacation that nobody would miss him while gone and that there might not even be a job left for him when he got back. He was onto a correct premonition. Some year, some day when we leave, we will not be missed very long and there will not be a job, a place for us when we come back. When we finally realize that we are indispensable only to God, it can be quite a relief, both to us and to those who (we think) depend upon us for their happiness. What a burden it is to be responsible for someone else's happiness! In fact, when the time came for Jesus to leave his friends, he said to them, "It is to your advantage that I go away, for if I do not go away, the Counselor will not come to you" (John 16:7). We are to cultivate the art of leaving, to ascertain the time and place of our leaving, and to entrust ourselves and others into the eternal care of God.

What do you say when you say goodby? Liv Ullmann writes in her book *Changing:*

"The man I was married to all those years ago was called Jappe. I am at his fortieth birthday party. I am not the hostess. I have been placed almost at the foot of the table. But from there I can better see the man I had lived with when I was very young. He is not as slim as he had been; he looks happier, but also more tired. His wife is everything that I was not. Part of it, perhaps, I could have become, if we had really tried. . . . There is much I remember and recognize, many threads at the table, in some of which I willingly entangle myself. But here are also deep chasms of strangeness. I look at Jappe and feel how fond I am of him and how good it is to know that he exists.

One day he comes with his little daughter to my summer cottage. She is two years old. They stroll together over the rocks and I stand by the window and look at them. No one sees me and I cry. He is holding her hand, pointing and explaining. Oh, so patiently. And she is small and safe with him. His smile is one I have never seen.

Many years ago when we had decided to be divorced, we sat holding hands in the marriage counselor's office. He asked why we wished to separate, if we were such good friends. "Just for that reason," we replied cheerily. We stood in the street and said goodby, because I was going to Ingmar in Sweden. And when we had no more cheerful words to say, we had nothing. At least nothing that ventured out. "Bye, then," he said and walked away. He never turned around. I turned all the time, just in case. . . . It was so strange to see him walk among all the other people. None of whom paid any attention to him. Only I knew who he was and what had happened to him. If I could have run after him, I would have done it. But my mouth could not speak; my feet could not walk in that direction.[5]

Sometimes there are no words for saying goodby. There are only memories and hopes and prayers.

Lord, I entrust now these dear persons to your care, in whose care they have been since their birth and will be beyond their death and my death. I leave them in your gracious hands as I go in your gracious hands. Care for me and for them. Let us

---

[5] Liv Ullmann, *Changing* (New York: Knopf, 1977), pp. 90–91.

find our own ways and let them be within your ways. As we separate and the ties unbind and the threads of our lives disentangle and we make ready for a new weaving, let us believe in our hearts that nothing we have shared together that is good will be lost, that all we were takes its honored place in our life's journey, that nothing is cancelled, but some things are settled and concluded, that much we cannot say or communicate, nonetheless abides and endures, that nothing can separate us from your love, in your love.

For me, leaving home meant having to hear others say "goodby" to me. I resigned from my parish shortly after moving out of my home and began the process of finding a new job. I thought there would be many interesting opportunities. Early in my search I took the train to see a friend of mine at an institution familiar to me and familiar with me. I thought I might like to do my midlife study there and that I could be useful to that institution in terms of my experience and competence in the ministry. Our appointment was for 9:00 in the evening. I waited in my hotel room for him. 9:00 came and went and then 9:30 and then 10:00. No phone call. I began to feel unwanted. Maybe I was damaged goods now. I didn't have a hat, but I began to feel as though I were holding one in my hand. I began to think he didn't want to see me. I finally went to his home to see if I had misunderstood the place of our meeting. As I stood in the vestibule of his house, I heard him talking with his wife upstairs. They had just gotten home. "Is he still waiting?" she asked. "Yes," he replied. "Well, don't be gone long." "I won't," he replied. He came down and we went back to my hotel and talked a while. There was no place in the institution for me. The institution was suffering a financial squeeze. Yes, he thought I could do a useful thing, but everybody was holding onto his job, and there was simply no money. Yes, it was too bad. What other possibilities did I have? I could see on his face that he pitied me. I felt that he wasn't really interested in me as a person or a professional. I felt angry and hurt and afraid. Mostly afraid. I had never had to go out and ask for a job before. Jobs had always come seeking me. It was chilling. It was a long and fearful train ride back to my apartment, not knowing where I was to go.

Herb Gardner's play *The Goodby People* lasted only about three weeks on Broadway, but it had some good scenes. In one, the "hero" is trying to raise money for a business venture. Everybody he calls is wary until they discover what he's after. Then they search for ways of saying "goodby." Their goodbys are warm and friendly. Finally to one of them the hero says, "You're lousy at saying 'hello' (*he imitates them, warily, with distance*) . . . allo? . . . who is it? . . . whaddy ya want? But you're great at saying 'goodby.' (*He imitates them: warm, palsy, solicitous*) . . . So long, buddy, take care, see ya . . . bye bye . . . love to the wife and kids . . . take it easy"—breezy and final.

I met a good many "goodby people" in the few months after leaving home. And I also met a few "hello people," people who listened, heard, and helped. One friend whom I hadn't seen for years called me long-distance one day. He said, "Hey, I hear things are moving and changing in your life. How are you? Tell me what's happening." So I told him, and he said to come see him, he understood what I was about, and that I needed to be on a new journey, and he valued me as a person and my competence as a clergyman. "Come and see me," he said. So I did. What a friend we have in anyone who seeks us out in a hard time and says in one way or another, "I care. I value you. You are valuable. There will be a way." There were others, important others, who said hello to me personally and professionally in that time, and they made a difference, a big difference.

Leaving home means going out not knowing. Abraham and Sarah had no map to the promised land, no inside track to discover the land of their inheritance. All they had was the promise of a presence on the journey and an earnest of meaning. So it is with us. In our faith journey we discover afresh that biblical faith is not knowledge. It is not having answers, but being driven and drawn by questions. Faith is not managing our destiny, but losing control of our destiny. Faith requires us to learn to trust the process. Faith is the pursuit of understanding and no longer of certainty. Faith is commitment without all the evidence being in. Faith is learning to trust God in the dark. Faith is losing some friends and gaining others. Faith is the fear of finding one's self in the hands of the living God. Faith is risk as well as promise, and darkness in the tunnel as well as the hope of light at the end of the tunnel.

Going out not knowing means moving into a time and place of vulnerability. I have long suffered from "agenda anxiety." When I get up in the morning, as part of my daily prayers I write down my agenda for the day. It comforts me just to see it take shape on the page. I'm a list maker, and I feel good as through the day I cross off the items that I have accomplished. "I make lists; therefore I am." I like to be in control of my life and have everything important to me secure and secured. I like the order that I myself design and maintain. But suddenly upon leaving home my "order" was broken and gone, and a frightening kind of disorder was in its place. The pieces were in the air, and not only could I not catch all of them as they came down, I couldn't even see many of them anymore. The only thing that was clear was that nothing was clear about my future. Once the structures that kept my life all together were removed, there was a ferment in the nucleus of my life. I knew in my head that every order is provisional, that life is contingent, that chaos lurks in every unit of order. But now I experienced the chaotic energies loose in my own self and life and in the systems to which I was attached. The demons were flying again, and I had to learn again, at my age, that I do not control my destiny, and at times may not even be able to manage it. In Saul Bellow's book *Humboldt's Gift*, Charlie Citrine reminds an overly optimistic friend, "The disorder is here to stay."[6] I believe it now. And I don't think I'll ever forget it again. I keep on wanting to stillphoto my life when things are going well. I want to keep it like that forever, protect it against every little death and against the big death. And I still try. But I really know it won't work, and that the disorder is here to stay, and the best I can do is cultivate my garden and hold the principalities and powers at bay a while. Nothing is safe forever, except all things, in the love of God. But the form of nothing will abide.

I learned the passing of the forms in so many ways. I passed out of friendships that couldn't or wouldn't sustain my new journey. I passed out of a church denomination that found consternation with me more pertinent than understanding, shelter, and restoration. As I felt myself to be further from some church people and church institutions, I felt closer to God, and especially closer to

---

[6] Saul Bellow, *Humboldt's Gift* (New York: Avon Books, 1974), p. 242.

Jesus. It amazed me that the institution claiming to embody the Spirit of Jesus, who was a magnet for people whose lives were broken and who in one way or another had become strangers, did not know how to welcome its own, much less strangers. A strange kind of reversal had taken place. Jesus offended the respectable self-righteous and in his presence the "sinners" felt comfortable. Yet, the Church of Jesus embraced the respectable and turned its face away from sinners. What a switch!

I had not needed shelter before. I had felt strong and able to handle my problems and my fears. But now I needed shelter. I needed safety. I could no longer have contempt for those who needed shelter because I needed it. I was reading the psalms in the Jerusalem Bible and came upon a number of psalms speaking of the author's need for shelter:

> Watch over my soul, rescue me;
> let me not be shamed: I take shelter in you.
> *Psalm 25:20*

> In you, Yahweh, I take shelter;
> never let me be disgraced. . . .
> Yahweh, how great your goodness,
>   reserved for those who fear you,
> bestowed on those who take shelter in you. . . .
> Inside your tent you shelter them
>   far from the war of tongues. . . .
> *Psalm 31:1, 19–20*

> In you, Yahweh, I take shelter. . . .
> Be a sheltering rock for me. . . .
> *Psalm 71:1, 3*

> If you live in the shelter of the Most High
> and make your home in the shadow of the God of
>   heaven,

you can say to the Lord, 'My refuge, my fortress,
my God in whom I trust!'

. . . .

He covers you with his feathers,
and you find shelter underneath his wings.
Psalm 91:1, 2, 4

How beautiful to come upon these psalms and to know
that I was yet in the company of those who believed and
hoped in God, that it was okay to need shelter, and that
God provided shelter for his people, even skins for Adam
and Eve in their time of going out not knowing, manna
for his people on their wilderness journey, and tents for
Abraham and Sarah when they left home.

In my childhood I learned a good many psalms by
heart. One summer the regimen was: "learn a psalm or a
portion of a psalm by heart and *then* you may have your
bottle of soda pop." Terrible pedagogy, but effective for
the learning of psalms by heart! I'm glad today for the
psalms that crept into my bones in those days and are now
available to me. I have my father to thank for that legacy.
In the times when I was most afraid, I looked around for
hills. "I will lift up mine eyes unto the hills, from whence
cometh my help. . . . My help cometh from the
Lord. . . . The Lord shall preserve thy going out and thy
coming in from this time forth, and even for evermore"
(Psalm 121:1-2, 8, KJV). The Lord will preserve your going
out—even your going out not knowing!—especially your
going out not knowing! Good news! Joy! Gospel! It was
time to grow up. Time to go on my own, without the
support of others if necessary, but confident in the support
of God, although hidden and silent much of the time.

In those days I discovered the poetry of Theodore

Roethke. He was like a contemporary psalmist to me, and sometimes I would read his poetry along with the scripture of the day, and sometimes one of his poems would become my prayer. One such is called "The Waking": [7]

I wake to sleep, and take my waking slow.
I feel my fate in what I cannot fear.
I learn by going where I have to go.

We think by feeling. What is there to know?
I hear my being dance from ear to ear.
I wake to sleep, and take my waking slow.

Of those so close beside me, which are you?
God bless the Ground! I shall walk softly there,
And learn by going where I have to go.

Light takes the Tree; but who can tell us how?
The lowly worm climbs up a winding stair;
I wake to sleep, and take my waking slow.

Great Nature has another thing to do
To you and me; so take the lively air,
And, lovely, learn by going where to go.

This shaking keeps me steady. I should know.
What falls away is always. And is near.
I wake to sleep, and take my waking slow.
I learn by going where I have to go.

[7] Theodore Roethke, "The Waking," *The Collected Poems of Theodore Roethke* (Garden City, N.Y.: Doubleday, 1975), p. 105.

3 | Living in Tents

By faith he sojourned in the land of promise, as in a
foreign land, living in tents with Isaac and Jacob, heirs
with him of the same promise.

Hebrews 11:9

*A*BRAHAM and Sarah found themselves sojourning in the wilderness. A *journey* is biblical prime time for being apprehended afresh by God. "That very day two of them were going to a village named Emmaus, about seven miles from Jerusalem, and talking with each other about all these things that had happened. While they were talking and discussing together, Jesus himself drew near and went with them" (Luke 24:13–15). "Now as he journeyed he approached Damascus, and suddenly a light from heaven flashed about him. And he fell to the ground and heard a voice saying to him, 'Saul, Saul, why do you persecute me?' " (Acts 9:3–4).

The *wilderness* is biblical prime place for being apprehended afresh by God. "Now Moses was keeping the flock of his father-in-law, Jethro . . . and he led his flock to the west side of the wilderness, and came to Horeb, the mountain of God. And the angel of the Lord appeared to him in a flame of fire out of the midst of a bush . . ." (Exodus 3:1–2). "In those days Jesus came from Nazareth

of Galilee and was baptized by John in the Jordan. And
when he came up out of the water, immediately he saw
the heavens opened and the Spirit descending upon him
like a dove; and a voice came from heaven, 'Thou art my
beloved Son; with Thee I am well pleased.' The Spirit
immediately drove him out into the wilderness" (Mark
1:9–11). God goes with us on our wilderness journeys.

A wilderness journey allows recovery of the natural. Being
on a wilderness journey means leaving the familiar, the
urbane, the cultivated and going out into the strange, the
primitive, the natural. Going from the domestic and the
tamed to the wild and untamed. It can mean this
movement in geographical, psychological, or theological
terms. For me, it literally meant leaving a metropolitan
ministry of twenty years and going into the "wilderness"
of a mountain retreat center. I came to Kirkridge Retreat
and Study Center in the fall of 1974 as Director. I began
getting back in touch with my own natural rhythm,
moving into accord with the season of my life cycle. I
found fresh awareness of my own creatureliness. Not only
am I a person in history, called to participate in the
movements of my own and my culture's history, but I am
a creature in the great chain of being, a creature with a
body, a mute yearning:

> I'd be beyond; I'd be beyond the moon,
> Bare as a bud, and naked as a worm.
>
>   .   .   .   .
>
> I would with the fish, the blackening salmon, and the mad
>   lemmings,
> The children dancing, the flowers widening.
> Who sighs from far away?
> I would unlearn the lingo of exasperation, all the distortions
>   of malice and hatred;

I would believe my pain: and the eye quiet on the growing
   rose;
I would delight in my hands, the branch singing, altering the
   excessive bird;
I long for the imperishable quiet at the heart of form;
I would be a stream, winding between great straited rocks in
   late summer;
A leaf, I would love the leaves, delighting in the redolent
   disorder of this mortal life,
This ambush, this silence,
Where the shadow can change into flame,
And the dark be forgotten.
I have left the body of the whale, but the mouth of the night
   is still wide. . . .[1]

With Roethke I have learned through many springs and
autumns to listen with a second ear for a sound like that of
many dogs yelping in the distance. When I hear it now,
my heart turns over, and I run out onto the deck and stare
into the eastern sky, until I see them again—a long wavy
V—several dozen Canadian geese winging their way
southward or northward, according to the season. It still
astonishes me, their haunting flight, their desperate joy. I
hearken to them, and for a moment I too am wild and on
the wing, moved by the hidden compass of my heart, in
tune with the rhythm of the universe, resonating with the
true north of my being and of all being.

   I look for our resident birds every morning: regular
visitors who feel at home with us, who cheep if the seed is
not there by 8:00 A.M.! Chickadees, juncos, jays, cardinals;
woodpeckers at the suet. In the spring there are

---

[1] Theodore Roethke, "The Longing," *The Collected Poems of Theodore Roethke*, p. 182.

goldfinches and purple finches, grossbeaks, towhees, and sometimes a flicker. For several weeks one autumn there was a sensational red-bellied woodpecker! I try to catch their songs and sing with them. I feel a kinship of grace and creation with them. My meditation is with them. Roethke speaks of the "littles" of the world, the "lovely diminutives." So it is with me. As I consider the birds of the air, my spirit is available and vulnerable to the Spirit. The natural is sacrament for me, vehicle of the momentary presence of God.

In these years I have found a new company of pilgrims, enjoying the wilderness journey with me and enriching my appreciation of its mysteries, beauties, and meanings. People like Lewis Thomas *(The Lives of a Cell)*, Annie Dillard *(Pilgrim at Tinker Creek)*, René Dubos *(A God Within)*, Loren Eiseley *(The Night Country)*, M. C. Richards *(Centering)*, William Warner *(Beautiful Swimmers)*, and Carl Sagan *(The Dragons of Eden)*[2] are contemporary psalmists for me. Their writings reflect a vast respect for the cosmos and this homeland earth, love for small creatures and the inconsiderables of the natural world, awe in the presence of the mystery of life and death and billions of years. Their questions are left hanging in humility, in a spirit like that of the psalmist, "When I consider the work of thy fingers, the moon and the stars, which thou hast ordained; what is man, that thou art mindful of him?" (Psalm 8:3-4, KJV).

---

[2] Lewis Thomas, *The Lives of a Cell* (New York: Viking, 1974); Annie Dillard, *Pilgrim at Tinker Creek* (New York: Harper's Magazine Press, 1974); René Dubos, *A God Within* (New York: Scribners, 1972); Loren Eiseley, *The Night Country* (New York: Scribners, 1971); M. C. Richards, *Centering* (Middletown, Ct.: Wesleyan University Press, 1962); William Warner, *Beautiful Swimmers* (New York: Penguin, 1977); Carl Sagan, *The Dragons of Eden* (New York: Random House, 1977).

Their writing nourishes my spirit and provides material for my meditation. I'm always on the lookout for this kind of author whom I do not know, and it is a great joy when I discover a new one.

A wilderness journey allows recovery of the simple. Such a journey speaks of deprivation, hunger, stripping down to essentials, being stripped of familiar creature comforts, and grieving losses. Yet at the same time it speaks of the cleansing clarity of a rushing wind blowing away the dead pieces of yesterday, clearing our musty lives of dead dust, and stinging our eyes with true bits of today whirring in the air. Heightened awareness. Senses cleaned. Inner voices sounding like bells. Colors and shapes on the changing screen of memory and hope.

Wilderness speaks of reducing our lives and life styles to a few sticks of furniture and some books and putting it on a move-it-yourself basis. For some time now, I've been getting along with one car instead of two. I'm into natural foods and eating less meat. I'm just scratching the surface of voluntary simplicity, seeking a lean life style, shedding things I don't need, struggling toward simple living. This stripping down is not only a cultural imperative, but for me it has something to do with my age, my time in the life cycle. Someone once put it this way: "The young laugh at the way things seem; middle age laughs at the way things are. The young want to dynamite the treasure vaults of life, middle age has learned the combination. The young think they know; middle age knows that no one knows. . . . Before forty, one adds and feeds to gorge the ego; after forty, one subtracts and simplifies to feed the soul."

Only in my mid-forties did I decide to stop gorging my ego and go through the pain, breakage, and fear required

for me to begin feeding my soul. I know there are many
who are about this simplification of life long before their
forties, many others long after, and some never! At
whatever age, the wilderness journey calls us to "a posture
of relinquishment," a life style where moth, rust, and theft
can't do much to your treasure, which is mainly in heaven,
and can't disturb your assets, which are chiefly inner.

A wilderness journey allows a recovery of solitude.
Aloneness, in which one is defining his own space and
savoring his own solitude and sculpting out the contours
of his own individuality. Loneliness, when there is the loss
of certain belonging; one knows he has left home and
hasn't arrived yet at another and that indeed there may not
be another, except for an oasis here and there along the
way. Privacy, in which the self is protected, gathered,
quieted so as to be ready at a later time for intimacy.
Silence. One begins to hear the silence when he is alone
for a time. The silence is a great teacher. Chaim Potok
wrote, "My father himself never talked to me, except when
we studied together. He taught me with silence. He taught
me to look into myself, to find my own strengths, to walk
around inside myself in company with my soul. When his
people would ask him why he was so silent with his son,
he would say to them that he did not like to talk, words
are cruel, words play tricks, they distort what is in the
heart, they conceal the heart, the heart speaks through
silence. One learns of the pain of others by suffering one's
own pain, he would say, by turning inside oneself, by
finding one's own soul."[3] A wilderness journey allows a
recovery of the natural and the simple out of solitude.

---

[3] Chaim Potok, The Chosen (New York: Simon & Schuster, 1967),
p. 278.

People on a wilderness journey are people living in tents.
Journeyers live in tents tentatively, in between the times,
in between homes. Journeyers learn to live with portable
roots that they can pull up from time to time, carry with
them, and plant again, like tent stakes, for a night or a
season. Journeyers follow an ambulatory God who never
stops anywhere for long, who can't be fenced in or out,
penned up or otherwise confined in doctrines or
institutions or any kind of ecclesiastical invention.

Living in tents means shedding roles and masks, sitting
loose to yesterday's agendas and prepackaged designs:
whether political, economic, theological, or ethical. Tents
are not meant to be permanent shelters; they are temporary
shelters that can be dismantled and reassembled quickly.
Tent dwellers know that no habitation abides, and that the
only question is when they will move on. Therefore, tent
dwellers do not take their structures, institutions, and roles
too seriously, nor do they take themselves too seriously.
Tent dwellers can no longer be devastated as they once
were when their first house was destroyed. Now they
know that any house can be destroyed, so they don't put
their trust in houses anymore. Tents will do quite well.

Living in tents speaks of transition, passage, change.
Our life cycle alternates in the rhythm of change and
continuity, mobility and stability. Alexander Calder's 1977
exhibit at the Whitney Museum in New York consisted of
his famous stabiles: those huge, steely structures rooted in
the floor, solidly planted on the ground, powerful
energies stretched taut and held fast in orange, blue,
yellow, and red. And there were also those delicately
designed floating creations called mobiles: afloat on air or
water, swinging by the rhythm of the universe, ever
moving, blowing in the wind, a circus of spontaneity and

serendipity. The exhibit reminded me that our lives move between periods of *stability:* where we have it all together, things are in order, under control, the systems and structures of our lives are fixed, nailed down, grounded— and periods of *mobility:* where things are separating, taking off, floating, pirouetting, flying, soaring; periods in which our roles and relationships are in glorious and terrible disarray, and it does not yet appear what we shall be tomorrow or next year. Mobility is the order of the day and night for those who are living in tents. We live toward a new stability, congruence, coherence; we are seeking a homeland. But we're not there yet. Now we are changing. We realize this poignantly in our middle years when we watch our parents aging and our children leaving home— in between the generations. Tents are an image of shifting roles, relationships, and meanings.

I have been living in tents with my parents. On a recent visit to my parents my father took me to the bank where my parents' valuable documents are kept in a safe deposit box. I am the executor of my parents' wills. We got out the box and went into the little stall provided for such business. As we stood there in that stall looking at the opened box, I had the feeling that my father wanted me to touch those documents, that somehow it would comfort him if I handled them. So I touched them, turned them over, considered them. I felt my father was comforted, and I was comforted too. And I also felt an early sorrow in the realization that one day I would stand in that stall with those documents alone. My father was rehearsing my parents' death. I was rehearsing my role in it. And indeed anticipating my own death.

I think of McDonald's breezy and phony TV commercial: "We do it all for you." The hell they do! They do it to make money for themselves. What we do is always mixed in motivation. Sometimes I resent the occasional implication from my parents that "you children are all we've got now. We live our lives through you. We fix up the summer cottage for your visits. We do it all for you." Part for us, but part also for themselves. We parents want our children to come see us and so we try to make it nice for them to come. But no child needs or wants the load of feeling that his parents depend upon him or her for the meaning of their lives. Gifts with emotional strings on them. We all give them and receive them in our families. The enormous emotional pull of parents. We have unique power to make our children feel guilty. Sam Keen spoke of this when he wrote about his parents, "Strong parents produce children who are destined either to conform to their values or to wage a fierce battle to escape the mold. I loved my parents; therefore I kill them in order to become myself."[4] And, when he writes of his children, "No doubt my son Gifford and my daughter Lael will do battle in the dark with faceless forces for half of their lifetime before they kick me out of their psyches. I hope I may live to see them celebrate independence day."[5]

It takes one to know one. I see myself as a parent wanting my children to write me letters and share their lives with me and tell me they love me. I came by such parenting honestly! I have files of letters written to me by my father during my two years in the Navy in World War II, my eight years in college and seminary, and in the years that followed. Affirming, nurturing letters. They

---

[4] Sam Keen, *Beginnings Without End* (New York: Harper & Row, 1975), p. 21.
[5] *Ibid.*, p. 129.

meant a lot to me, allowed and encouraged me to share my new experiences and thoughts with my parents. I knew my mother cared too, but it was my father who wrote. Those letters kept reminding and reassuring me that I was loved. And yet, there was also a not-so-hidden agenda in them. "Show your gratitude by writing back, often, weekly." So, I was taught to write my parents once a week as my father wrote me once a week, as he wrote his parents once a week. Even so, I want my four children to write me if not once a week, at least often.

What is it with my father and me? Is it that I am so much like him, that I can see my own ambivalences in his and don't like to be reminded so graphically of the ambiguities in my own fathering?[6] Or, is it that I am still reacting against the powerful role model he was for me in order to maintain my own dignity and integrity? The mingling of affection and anger, of love and indifference. We are different, he and I, maybe chiefly different as our generations are different. A friend wrote me about his struggle with his father:

> I continue to meet with a counselor who is working to help me to be set free from the legalistic bindings imposed by parents, church, culture, etc. The anger I had toward those institutions is being swallowed up by my realization that the tendency in me that allowed the binding is also able to unwrap the bonds. For example: My father taught me to have a rigid view of the Sabbath. He doesn't go for the idea that I have season tickets to the Steelers. The other night he said over the phone: "You know I don't approve of going to

---

[6] See Edward F. Stein, ed., *Fathering: Fact or Fable* (Nashville, Tenn.: Abingdon, 1977) for a useful investigation of the meanings of fathering and being fathered.

football games on Sunday." I responded before I even thought: "Then I don't think you ought to go," and was delighted with my answer.

In the summer of 1977, while visiting my parents in Michigan, I received proposed advertising copy for my book *Living the Questions*. The copy was:

Ever since I've been
Living life's questions

I've been finding
God's answers.

I felt uncomfortable with that. I don't claim to be finding God's answers. I don't think anybody finds *God's* answers. We get hints and clues now and then. But I believe, rather, that I am finding my own provisional answers for my own life's questions and that the point is to *live* the questions in the knowledge that all answers are provisional. So, I revised the copy to read:

The point is not to
find answers

But to
live questions.

But my father liked the original statement and said, "People would be very grateful if they felt you could help them to find God's answers for their lives. If you aren't providing God's answers, whose answers are you providing?" The implication was that my job, as a clergyman, was to provide *God's* answers and that *my* answers were surely suspect. I think my father and I would agree that life consists of both questions and answers. Perhaps he would emphasize the answer dimension and I the question dimension. And perhaps that is the major difference between us: theologically, ethically, generationally? I don't know. I only know that my parents and I live in tents and that we always will, and that it's all right. There will be no closure, no agreement, no arrival, no cessation. As long as we all live and maintain our integrity, we will live in tents and exchange such tokens of affection and respect as we can.

Indeed, the roles may shift from offspring-parent, or adult-adult, to offspring parenting parent. And for some of us, just as our children are leaving home, our parents are arriving home again, needing our attention. "Dad, you mustn't drive the car if your vision is impaired." "Bob, I can see well enough!" Being able to drive a car spells mobility, independence, the way things have been and are meant to be, life! Not being able to drive a car spells dependence, being stuck, the way things are not meant to be, death! "Dad, I don't think you should go out in the sailboat alone and expose yourself to the possibility of tipping over and the trauma of having to climb back aboard and right the boat." "Bob, I want to participate, not be a spectator. I want to do everything I can do safely and wisely." I must understand and moderate even as I try to persuade and let be. It is painful to grow old. It is painful to watch loved ones grow old. It is painful to be living in those tents, but necessary, and it's all right.

I hear the piano playing in the basement of my parent's cottage. The old gospel hymns, my father's voice singing. I go down and stand behind my father. My mother joins him on the piano bench. We sing the gospel hymns. My hands on my father's shoulders, his white hair. My father. My mother. His stiff fingers on the piano. The myriad lines in my mother's face. I love them.

I have been living in tents with my children. The children have been leaving home now for many years. Two years ago my youngest daughter received early admission to college. She's strong, independent, half woman, half little girl. She's passionate about her life, self-righteous, knows just what she wants to be about. I know something of where she comes from. I wrote her a letter outlining her responsibilities at college in what I felt to be a gracious, kind, indeed magnanimous manner. A long typewritten letter came back by return mail, part of which read:

"I feel the need to claim my personhood and separateness from you and Mom. I need to be on my own and have my own *separate* identity. When I read your letter over, I saw how much of it was parenting and advice. Very insistent advice. You care for me a lot . . . and want me to take advantage of my opportunities and potential. . . . I do too!!!! I am part of you in the sense that you shaped my basic opinions and beliefs, but beyond that I am totally mine and I claim that. You have prepared me for the journey. I am begging and at the same time insisting to be unleashed. . . . Don't worry unreasonably for me. I am going to experience as much as possible and I'm going to love every minute of it. I feel so close to you and that really feels good. It also frees me. Thanks for being such a good father. Now, be my friend. I invite you to take part in my life as a friend. . . . Lots of love, reassurance, and support. . . . Your daughter and friend, Nancy."

Sometimes I do worry about my daughter and friend, whether unreasonably or not I don't know. I continue to be a paying friend! I respect her insistence on shaping her own life. I'm having to learn to wait for the Lord with my daughter, having to let her be and let her go on her own journey, having to let her pitch her tent wherever she chooses and make her choices and her mistakes and have her victories and defeats and just wait for her with the bandages and ointments ready.

My brother once said of our own childhood, "We were programmed for repetition, not self-discovery." Have I programmed my children for repetition, not self-discovery? Do I want them to be like me, to take my value system and my life style and make it their own? Am I pleased with them when they make the choices I made and value what I value? Yes. Am I willing to credit them for making choices different from mine, and for stepping to the drumbeat they hear, strange as it may sound to my ears? I want to. I hope they will remember me on my birthday, Father's Day, and at other special times. It surprises me that I do want them to and that it hurts a little when they don't. Why should I think I am exempt from the need to be remembered by my children? If I am beyond being vulnerable to them, I am beyond being emotionally accessible to them. Already, like my parents, I too need attention to be paid to me. I too want to be appreciated. I want to participate in my children's lives. And if I don't do it all for them, I do some of it for them.

The tents move and shift. I am pleased when my son Bob talks proudly with me about his name, his being a Junior. It comforts me that now he wants to be identified with me, his father. I know in my head that he will need to disidentify with me, his father, before many years pass. I hope I will handle that with understanding, but I feel the loss already in my stomach. I want to be able to sit loose and watch him go, gladly. It remains to be seen and heard and touched and felt and tasted. Our intention as parents is often better than our performance.

My eldest daughter Cathy pleases me in the ways I

taught her to please me, elder son that I was. Dutiful, responsible, considerate, funny, getting good grades, working, supporting herself. One of the songs in the black musical *The Wiz* is called, "Don't Give Me No Bad News!" I've been singing that song to my children over the years. Cathy shares her life in great and colorful detail and delights in bringing "good" news because she knows how it pleases me. Mea culpa! My middle daughter, Barbara, struggles to kick me out of her psyche, and at the same time communicates a loyal love for me that abides. I know I can go to her for comfort when I am scared or sad and she will be there for me, because she already has been more than once. She is generous, compassionate, explosive, filled with laughter and with some pain, too. She has come into her own responsible autonomy, working, pursuing her education, and taking responsibility for her life. I feel the warmth of her caring. Barb said to me last summer, "On the way to the airport I noticed the wrinkles in Mom's face, and it made me sad. Yesterday, when you were lying on the dock, I saw the wrinkles in your face, and it made me sad." She is sad about the aging and signs of death of her parents. But she is also sad about her own aging, the experience of being alone, and the need to take responsibility, unprotected and on her own. The transitions of others significant to us trigger our awareness of our own transitions.

I have been living in tents with Cindy. She came into my office at First Community Church of Columbus, Ohio, one day in the spring of 1971. We were to design and prepare a worship service together. She had been recommended as an articulate, imaginative woman competent in the design of worship. So she was. But more, much more. Direct of bearing, clear of eye, focused in mind, and at ease in her body, I saw her—a woman of quiet grace and erotic mystery. I was stunned. We did our work. Months passed. Occasionally there were smiles of recognition across a hall—recognition of what? Casual conversation between us began to carry an uneasy, electric intensity.

Cindy was born, raised, and educated in Liberty, Missouri. She writes,

> I am a child of the American Middle West, an authentic WASP, which for me means white, Anglo-Saxon, Presbyterian. I came from an Emily Dickinsonian mother: private and independent, yet sheltered, duty-bound, intellectual, critical, and strong in faith. I came from a Swiss father: gentle and rough-hewn, full of humor, warmth, and stubborn devotion; strong in humility, simplicity, and faith. I was taught: tend to your own business, do not ask for help, trust in the Lord, contain your negative feelings, things will always be as they are, things are as they were meant to be, do your duty.

It was to be the way of true grit. She holds special childhood memories of her small town . . . honeysuckle, daisy chains, scout camp, July 4th with the neighborhood, cedar waxwings in the spring, and one solitary hawthorne tree in the front yard of the house on the hill. Love of the earth, and of earth colors, darkly sensuous and rich.

Cynthia Hirni. Her father calls her Cynthia. In his old age they are close in love and respect. Her mother has been dead now for five years. There is still much unfinished business in their relationship. Cindy grieves a glad, warm closeness that never was, and struggles to understand a severity that made her wary, cautious, and skeptical, although it did not cripple her femininity or sense of self-worth. In my view Cindy individuated early in order to become her own person under critical eyes. As a teacher of English and French to high school students, a wife and mother of two children, a responsible participant in civic, church, and social concerns, she became an integrated woman in her mid-thirties.

Cindy and I fell in love. "Fell" is the word and was the experience. We were apprehended by a power of need, recognition, and longing that would not go away, would not be stilled, but demanded attention and mandated a new future, together. Our readiness for each other reflected lack of fulfillment and badness of fit in our marriages. During those years of disentanglement from yesterday, fiercely affirming the rightness of today, while seeking to shape a viable tomorrow, fear, guilt, hope, subterfuge, courage, sadness, and joy seethed and tore us. We did not want to hurt others or be damaged ourselves. We wanted to be responsible both to external obligations and internal loyalties. We couldn't make it happen sinlessly or painlessly. It was painful for our former spouses, our children, our congregation, our friends, and for us in the time of passage. But there were also moments of great beauty, astonishing bits of understanding along with stern judgments, amazing gifts of personal and institutional grace.

We are making it. And over the years those close to us in love and responsibility are making it too. Healing and health and wholeness have blessed us. We began our married life together when we came to Kirkridge in the autumn of 1974, and we have been living in tents ever since. She has her tent, I have mine, and we both share one. Rilke wrote of "the love that consists in this, that two solitudes protect and border and salute each other."[7] We have seen on a number of occasions a male and female

---

[7] Rainer Maria Rilke, *Letters to a Young Poet*, trans. M. D. Herter Norton (New York: Norton, 1934), p. 59.

cardinal exchanging seeds. It is beautiful and simple. As it appears to me, the male cardinal gets the seed in his beak and flies to the female. They stand on the branch together, side by side. She turns her beak, he turns his beak, and he gives her the seed and she receives it. Eiseley wrote about the event:

> Here on my window ledge
> two cardinals,
> male and female,
> having lived alone all winter
> in that silence of the solitary
> who seek their own food
> and depend on no one,
> suddenly exchange seeds
> in an ancient ritual
> welcoming spring.
> They are not too intimate,
> the horn of the beak preventing.
> They are very wild
> but grave and dignified—
> at this moment
> so much so that if I could
> with the proper manners
> I should like to give
> a seed to you.[8]

(I took chauvinist comfort in the male giving the gift and the female receiving the gift, until one day Cindy pointed out to me two female cardinals exchanging seeds!)

The horn of the beak preventing: the hard edge of individuality, the boundary, the limit, the contoured self that will not be overrun, impinged upon, or invaded

---

[8] Loren Eiseley, "The Cardinals," *Notes of an Alchemist* (New York: Scribners, 1972), p. 93.

without protest and defense. We make a good match, we two. I am too trusting, she is too wary. I say more than I mean, she means more than she says. I overstate, she understates. She resists my agendas, I provoke hers. She prolongs my decisions, I hasten hers. We have the gift of intimacy, sometimes. I want to still-photo it, bottle it, wrap it up, preserve it. She wants to wait for it, notice it, get along without it, trust its return. We respect one another's privacy, usually. If intimacy is the sharing of privacies, the private self needs nourishment and respect. She tends her plants silently in the morning. I feed my birds and write in my journal silently in the morning. We are both meditating, separately.

We fight. She is stubborn. I am insistent. A wall goes up. There is an impasse, a chasm, a gulf that sometimes seems very wide. We fight over the children, lovemaking, our roles at Kirkridge. We wait. We suffer. There is a smile, a touch, a breath, a movement toward each other. We can talk again. We can touch again. We are all right.

Making love is, for me, a doorway of intimacy, opening into a spacious place of ease and grace and truth. I used to think that people need to talk and develop their closeness, and then make love as a climactic expression of their intimacy and go to sleep out of such communion. And that is nice. I also have found that making love can open windows of seeing and being seen and doors for going out and coming in, together. Making love can free us to become vulnerable again, tender, without agenda, able to share intimacy. Moments of great grace. You might say we share a kinship of grace.

When it came to preparing marriage vows for our wedding, we struggled, argued, and laughed as we sought to be as honest and real in those words as we could be. We chose to articulate some mutual values around honesty, growth, sharing, respecting, forgiving. The word "seeking" was important to us, expressing our deep hope and intention, but also acknowledging out of our own experience that no one can make guarantees.

Spouses deal differently with changing life patterns. I have friends in an eastern city. The woman was elected mayor of that city. She wrote about her and her husband's changing life patterns. "Otherwise I'm off on a roller coaster which proceeds at a breakneck pace from 8:30 A.M. Monday 'til 5:00 P.M. Friday. Weekends are for house cleaning and speech writing. At times it's maddening, and at other times it's tremendously satisfying. Don [her husband] is bearing up well. He is of the generation and temperament to yearn for a full-time wife, mother, and a well-appointed home and tasteful meals attended by respectful children, polished off by a good backrub and whatever else may follow. I don't blame him. I yearn for the same thing. I tell him, what we both need is a wife!" Those people are working out their changing patterns constructively. Others aren't so patient, creative, or well matched.

I have been living in tents with my ministry. I am comfortable now in my role as Director of Kirkridge, the retreat and study center which I'll discuss more in Chapter 5. It is both a job and a ministry. Eighteen years ago, when I was thirty-four years old, I wrote in my first book, *New Life in the Church,* with some scorn, about the fact that some people get tired in their ministries and come to think of their work as a job instead of a ministry. At that time, my identity *was* my vocation. There was no distance between myself and my role. Now at fifty-two, I perceive and experience my occupation as both a job and a ministry, an occupation and a vocation. It is a job in terms of my specific responsibilities and functions. It is a ministry in terms of my relationships and my capacity to be human in my roles. It is less hortatory, less manipulative than in the past. Part of that is due to my own growth, and part is due to the nature of the relationships I have in this role. My relationship with retreatants is not usually heavy, either for them or for me. I have little power over them. They don't pedestal me. I don't solicit them. I wear my role lightly, most of the time. I feel that my role constricts less than it used to my capacity to be real. The person and the profession seem to be in good focus; the eye can see clearly through the lens. It is a comfortable fit.

Currently Cindy searches for a new vocational self-definition apart from me and Kirkridge. The isolation of our mountainside, although nourishing in privacy and beauty, limits both educational and employment opportunities. There is freedom for her in not having a full-time job but frustration in serving an auxiliary role. Her friendship, civic, and social involvements are also limited by virtue of prime energy and time commitments at Kirkridge. My work is fulfilling for me. I enjoy Cindy's nearness and our ability to go away together as well as to share much of the work of Kirkridge together. If I am content in our tent, she is questioning and questing. We seem able to dwell in our different places with a measure of grace, honesty, and humor, bonded by considerable love and respect.

Being a clergyman is analogous in some respects to being an actor or actress because both types have public performance as central in their roles. Ellen Burstyn was interviewed once about her role in the movie *Alice Doesn't*

Live Here Anymore. She said, "With other characters I've had to wear a wardrobe. With Alice I could use my own skin. . . . In [Lee] Strasberg's training you learn to become strong enough to let your inner life show, which of course includes weaknesses." Whatever our occupational role, when we have courage to shed our robes and use our own skin with people—employees, employer, constituents, peers—and have enough strength to let our inner life show, then we connect with the vital humanity of others and the power of Spirit is released among us. Wherever there is significant power differential among fellow workers and colleagues, the capacity for unfearful and nonmanipulative friendship is limited if not crippled. Even so, and within those limitations, honest community can exist and develop. How good it is to be able to use my own skin in my job and ministry.

I am living in tents with relations and friends. I am rediscovering my brotherhood. What it is. What it isn't. A warm, intimate fellowship with one brother; a respectful and caring engagement with another brother; a realization of a lack of intimacy with my sister and new, satisfying outreaches to each other. Somehow it all matters to me more. As parents die and children leave home, other relatives and friends become more needed. The Christmas-card list suffers attrition and addition. As we change, our friendships change: some endure, others fade, new ones are born. Friendship on the journey. Friendship on the run. A number of friends and colleagues come to lead a retreat for us every year or two. Sometime ago I wrote one such friend in preparation for his next event. The last paragraph of my letter read: "Early hearth fires here, snow flakes already, how beautiful it is on our mountain. In former days we would have felt guilty for feeling so happy. Now we simply rejoice and know that nothing is forever." He wrote me back a couple weeks later, dealt with the business he had to conduct with me, and then said, "The last paragraph of your letter cut right through my morning business. It's the day before Thanksgiving. I'm rushing to get through so that I can be with the family over the holidays. Your letter just cut through that nonsense and reminded me of the pain and joy of my life in these days, the uncertainties that surrounded me, how good life is, and how necessary are friends like you and some others who sustain me and whom I help sustain. Thanks for that most of all." Friendship on the run, in letters, over the phone, in thought and prayer, and once in a while celebrated in person. Gifts galore!

I observe others living in tents, moving painfully and hopefully through their own transitions. Georges Simenon, the French author, published a book of diaries, *When I Was Old*,[9] when he was sixty-seven. The diaries were written ten years earlier, when Simenon was fifty-seven and fifty-eight years old. It was in those years that he began to *feel* old. He was assailed with self-doubts, and he wondered if life had any more value for him, if he had any more value for life. Who would miss him when he died? Who would remember him? Who would care that he was gone? He became preoccupied with questions of legacy and unfinished business. He began to keep diaries of his feelings, and over a period of two years he moved through his passage from middle adulthood into the beginnings of later adulthood. He found that he was through the passage and out the other side and into a most satisfying and

---

[9] Georges Simenon, *When I Was Old* (New York: Harcourt Brace Jovanovich, 1970).

creative older adulthood. His diaries reveal a man needing reassurance that he was still somebody, that he still mattered to people close to him. He needed recognition and honoring even more than during the years when so much of it came to him. He wanted his children to know him in his vulnerability, his sins, his real self. He wanted them to take him off the pedestal and to realize that they might become better human beings than he had been. He found himself feeling at times like a stranger in the world.

Liv Ullmann writes of her seventeenth year when she left school and tried out as an actress at the school in Trondhjem.

> After my audition—Juliet and Ophelia—I stood in a corridor and waited for the list to be posted, of those who had been accepted. And when it happened a tall, awkward boy placed himself next to me and read aloud the names of the chosen ones. . . . Something was dying within me, because I was not included. . . . I stood in the corridor a long time until at last I knew all ten names by heart. . . . I walked out into the street. I walked all night, shocked and with a foreboding that this was the way my life would always be. . . . Then I only had Grandma. By morning I was with her, and I cried my heart out. Sobbed on a breast which never had harbored the dream that now was crushed within me. In the span of a night everything that was customary and familiar had been stripped away, and I was in the middle of a transition. There was something to be learned from this, something hard to understand: that one carries one's fate within oneself, one's fate is not dependent on this kind of failure or success. To become conscious is a long process, to become open to sorrow, look upon it as part of living, of developing, of changing.[10]

---

[10] Liv Ullmann, *Changing*, pp. 73–74.

Whether one is seventeen, thirty-seven, or fifty-seven, whatever the passage of transition, whether that of adolescence, middleescence, elderescence, the time of living in tents is painful in the loss of our yesterdays and filled with promise for our tomorrows. Transition can mean transformation. Those who are living in tents can be reborn.

How do we keep in touch with our deep self, with God, when we are living in tents? How do we pray? Many people are rediscovering the value of keeping a journal. For some people, an intensive journal, highly structured and rational. For others, a casual journal in which one may make entries from time to time. Whatever the intensity or casualness, a journal is a means of articulating one's tenting experiences and keeping a record of them. Journals are an attempt to perceive the meanings in one's living and to surface the insights and to record the memories. Jung wrote, "Among all my patients in the second half of life—that is to say, over thirty-five—there has not been one whose problem in the last resort was not that of finding a religious outlook on life . . . (although) this of course has nothing to do with a particular creed or membership of a church."[11] A religious outlook, a framework of meaning, a clarification of value—journal writing helps in such a search. Quiet solitude in the morning is a mode and mood, a time and timing, when my spirit heals, insights appear, energy gathers, hope takes fresh wing. Watching the birds, reading the psalms. I have confidence in the spirituality of the psalmists and psalms. The psalms are earthed, grounded, honest, laden with

<hr>

[11] Carl Jung, *Modern Man in Search of a Soul* (New York: Harcourt Brace Jovanovich, 1933), p. 229.

power and feeling, and usually do not have doctrinal, evangelistic, or ethical agendas as central to their thrust. They are prayers and often trigger my praying. I do some journal writing nearly every morning. In a leisurely manner, not by a precise and rigorous exercise. I respect those who take their journals more seriously and perhaps derive more depth of insight from them. But my pietistic, rule-oriented background has left me skeptical of the enduring value, for me, of *any* spiritual methodology, system, or technique. My Jacob-journey wrestling with God in recent years has left me content, for a season, to wait for the Lord in my praying, to await the jostling and gentling of my spirit by the Spirit and to go with its flow.

Scattered through the pages of my journal is the phrase, "I praise you for another day free of pain in my left arm." A few years ago I developed soreness in my left arm. Tests revealed that I have (it sounds terrible!) arthritic disintegration of a vertebra in the back of my neck. For about two years, at intervals of a few months, the pain would come, stay for several weeks, and eventually depart. During the pain periods I wore a soft cervical collar to bed at night. One night I got up, had to go to the bathroom, stumbled in, turned on the light, and as I passed the mirror happened to see myself. I turned and looked full face in horror. There I was, wrinkled face, puffy eyes, with this *thing* around my neck. I shuddered to myself, "It's going to get me." And it will, someday. Or something else will. My life is circumscribed. So I learned, in the pain-free periods, to praise God for another day free of pain in my left arm. I know, of course, that tomorrow the pain will return, or some other pain. I will need in the painful periods to plumb the depths of praising God in the pain and beyond it.

So I wait and look and listen and jot and think and pray and smile and sometimes cry a little. I have to struggle to keep my list-making and agenda-making in its place, either before or after my journal time, and not in the middle of it. Waiting for the Lord is letting the momentum of my life and my context move with its own energy, discerning meaning here and perceiving insight there, letting the meanings gather, sift, sort, settle, come clear, or stay cloudy. Sometimes writing a prayer that grows out of the waiting, sometimes noting a task that claims attention, sometimes just being there, waiting for inner transformation. This is an attentive rather than an aggressive mode of praying for me. It is a "let it happen" instead of a "make it happen" kind of praying. The movement, for me, is a healthy one. It acknowledges the limits of my life and the boundaries of my existence. There is intentionality, but part of it is to prepare to observe the initiatives of the Spirit and be supple to them. It is the difference between planting a seed and nurturing the growth of the plant. Daily journaling is a nurturing of my spirit and feeding of my soul. It is a good way to pray for people living in tents.

Living in tents is the way of this world, the way of the pilgrim journey, the way of waiting until the day comes when our strength is renewed and we mount up with wings like eagles, ready to be reborn.

4 | Being Reborn

By faith Sarah herself received power to conceive,
even when she was past the age, since she considered
him faithful who had promised.

Hebrews 11:11

S*ARAH* received power to conceive. Power to conceive new being, new future, new life. Sarah embodies the female power of transformation, the mystery of generativity, the capacity of woman to yield new life of her own body. Her physical undergoing of the process of birth affords direct analogy to the process of rebirth. Sarah is a paradigm of what it means for us to be reborn.

Being reborn comes by recovering the feminine dimension of God. Virginia Mollenkott, in her book *Women, Men and the Bible,* explores the feminine aspects of God. She reminds us that Jesus pictures himself as a mother hen longing to gather its brood under her wings (Matthew 23:37), describes God as a woman who has lost one of ten coins and rejoices when she finds the lost coin (Luke 15:8-10), and speaks of the Spirit as being the agent of new birth (John 3:5-8). (The term Spirit in the Hebrew, *ruach,* is feminine.) Professor Mollenkott mentions a number of other passages to demonstrate that God is given both male and female representation in the Bible, and concludes, "If ever there was a picture of an *androgynous* God—a God who possesses both male and female characteristics—this is such a picture. The point, of course, is not that we are to see God as literally androgynous but that we are to recognize that God transcends the limitations of human sexuality." [1] Because most of us have had such a male-paternal image of God, it is important that we be able to experience and incorporate the feminine dimension of God.

For me to incorporate in myself the feminine dimension of God, I have needed to reappropriate my experience of my mother. I have not written much about her in this book. My father was a powerful male-paternal image of God for me, outshining my mother's presence. And yet my mother has always been there for me as a stable, strong, warm, and loyal presence. I have felt unconditionally affirmed by her from my earliest memories. She seemed to have a kind of glorious "my son right or wrong" prejudice in my behalf. As I wrote her this past year to help celebrate her eightieth birthday, I realized afresh that she is my major "balcony" person, to use Carlyle Marney's phrase. A balcony person is someone in your cheering section. My mother has been sitting in my cheering section, front row center, all my life. My father has been there too, next to her, with paternal expectation, challenge, and judgment. Regarding the "nurture and admonition of the Lord," both came from my father, and from my mother chiefly nurture. I am only now recognizing how important she was to my development of self-confidence. She offered me a nurturing embodiment of God.

---

[1] Virginia Ramey Mollenkott, *Women, Men and the Bible* (Nashville, Tenn.: Abingdon, 1977), p. 57. (Chapter Three, "Is God Masculine?" provides scholarly analysis of this issue.)

Imagining God in feminine terms allows my experience of God to be permeated by my feelings from and for my mother. She provided a personal, live-in relationship embodying the grace of God. As I allow this feminine imagery to transform my understanding and experience of God, I am experiencing feelings of security and safety, warmth and acceptance. I find myself shielded under her wings. God becomes something more than a Calvinist or Wesleyan caller to arms. She also offers everlasting arms on which it is all right, when necessary, to lean. Maternal and erotic dimensions of the being of God impact me, ambush me. I am comforted, nourished, intrigued. God is more mysterious, more transformative, more warmly available to me.

In the wrenching, soaring play *For Colored Girls Who Have Considered Suicide When The Rainbow is Enuf*, a young black woman sings out:

i found god in myself
i loved her/i loved her fiercely.[2]

A young man wrote about God searching for her lost coin (Luke 15:8–10):

Lighting a candle,
she throws yellow joy
into dark corners
and paints hope imagery
on dim walls.

Arming herself with broom,
she sweeps a way for wind to dance
and brushes a path for air to walk.

---

[2] Ntozake Shange, *For Colored Girls Who Have Considered Suicide When the Rainbow Is Enuf* (New York: Macmillan, 1977), p. 63.

Wearing Torah apron
and story scarf,
Mother Yahweh whisks
til Drachma lost
sleeps found in coin commune
and covenant purse.[3]

God is like a woman who hides leaven in three
measures of flour (Matthew 13:33) so that it may all be
leavened. It is the grace of Mother Yahweh hiding in the
dark confusion of our lives, quietly but inexorably
permeating our hopes. When we experience the Sarah in
God, we too receive power to conceive new being, new
future. Being reborn comes by recovering the feminine
dimension of God.

*Being reborn comes by recovering the feminine dimension of
ourselves.* According to the theory of Carl Jung, every man
and woman has both masculine and feminine qualities.
Our male-dominated culture programs boys to emulate
masculine qualities and girls to emulate feminine qualities,
overvaluing the masculine and undervaluing the feminine.
So it is necessary for both men and women to recover and
honor their feminine dimension.

Recovering my feminine dimension has meant
realizing that if I have tears it is all right for me to shed
them. It is not unmanly for me to cry. It is not unmanly
for me to let my sensitivity, feeling, tenderness, and
vulnerability emerge. These are feminine dimensions of
my being. If I crush or deny them, I am killing the
feminine parts of myself, emulating a macho, superjock
masculinity. If my masculine dimension emphasizes *doing,*
my feminine dimension emphasizes *being.* I have been

---

[3] Dean Stroud, "Mother Yahweh," unpublished poem..

coming into my own capacity to be, to enjoy, to yield, to bear inner fruit. I am allowing the Sarah as well as the Abraham in me to live. I am looking for feminine models in the Bible, as well as masculine ones, to yield insight and enrichment.

One result of this new look has been growing appreciation of Mary, the mother of Jesus. I used to look with some scorn upon people, usually Roman Catholics, who venerated Mary. Although I might continue to have *theological* differences regarding the role of Mary in the drama of redemption, in *psychological* terms those Catholics knew what they were doing! Mary embodies the feminine dimension of God and makes God more available, accessible, nurturing, accepting.[4] I am recognizing Mary now as my sister under the skin. The Mary in me is beginning to live. I identify with the event when Mary is visited by the angel Gabriel, overwhelmed, overshadowed, taken by surprise (Luke 1:26–38). At first she is afraid, and questions the possibility of the predicted birth. But finally she is reassured and says, "Let it be to me according to your word."

I often use that phrase as a prayer:

O Lord, let it be to me,
in this relationship or meeting,
according to your word;
let it be to my daughter, my son, my wife,
according to your word;
let it be to my job, my friend,
my neighbor, my enemy . . .
according to your word.

---

[4] See Robert A. Johnson, *He* (New York: Harper & Row, 1974), pp. 62–63.

When I allow the Mary in me to emerge, I am more able to be sensitive to the initiative of God. Sometimes I am given the capacity to respond to events that are initiated by others without resenting or competing. Sometimes I am able to be receptive, discerning, observing, noticing.

Roethke writes, "I recovered my tenderness by long looking."[5] When we let the Mary in us live we may be able to move from aggressive competition toward cooperation. We may be able to "look long" at the beauty of a mountain or a face, appreciate it for what it is in itself, and not need to take it and remake it in our own image or market it. The Mary in us may make us no less decisive but more responsive, no less strong but more vulnerable. It is the Mary in Roethke who releases him to exclaim, "Being, not doing, is my first joy."[6] Yes! The joy of being allows healing to happen and recollection to take place. In the morning when I sit sipping my coffee and watching our birds at the feeders, I seldom feel guilt at such "loafing" but enjoy a centering of my being, a quieting of my self, and a clarifying of my life.

The joy of being allows me to get in touch with my power to conceive, the power to create out of my own experience the stuff that dreams are made of and from which visions burst forth. I begin to understand why Eastern religions, especially Buddhism, emphasize being in their religious practice. I better understand the Quaker emphasis on waiting for the Lord in silence, without a constant profusion of words or flurry of activity. Being is a

---

[5] Theodore Roethke, "What Can I Tell My Bones?" in *The Collected Poems of Theodore Roethke*, p. 167.

[6] "The Abyss," *ibid.*, p. 214.

form of obedience with which I am comfortable. My self-understanding and my relationship with others and with God begin to change as I allow my feminine side to emerge.

I am recognizing the need to move from a primarily paternal relationship to other people toward a more mutual one. Because my images of God and myself were heavily masculinized in childhood, like my father I developed a paternal role in relation to the special people in my life without realizing it. As a clergyperson my professional role was paternal. I was a shepherd, guardian . . . warden? I was paternal toward Peg, with negative results for each of us. I was paternal toward many of my colleagues and friends, distancing them and often preventing personal intimacy. I was paternal toward my younger brothers and even my older sister. Only in the last few years have my brothers and sister and I been able to begin recovering our kinship. I realize today that women were undervalued in our home, as in many homes at that time. Part of that took the form of undervaluing my sister, not respecting her in the same way I learned to respect my male siblings. It was no coincidence that the three boys in our family were encouraged to go into the ministry, but not the one girl.

I am discovering especially how much I missed through the years in my remote relationship with my sister. As I shed the paternal role, it is possible for new relationship to develop between her and me. We are reaching out tentatively, carefully to each other, and beginning to develop a *mutual* friendship as brother and sister. A fire that almost went out is being rekindled. I am learning what it means to be in mutual relationship with my spouse and my brothers and to move from a paternal role with my children toward reciprocal relationships. Being reborn comes by recovering the feminine dimension in ourselves.

Being reborn comes by recovering the feminine dimension of the Church. In recent years I have been privileged to watch many church people beginning to recover the feminine dimension of their church experience. At one retreat a theologian spoke of the waves of new students coming to his seminary in recent years: Catholics, blacks, women, Jews, evangelicals, the New Age religionists. He related how each wave has disturbed, altered, and enriched the student body and the religious climate of the seminary. He said that the most profoundly disturbing new presence for him was the women. The women are requiring him to re-evaluate the history of Christian theology, which was written, of course, almost exclusively by the church *fathers.* Just as history written by whites does not do justice to blacks, so "male" theology does not do justice to female experience and presence in the history of the Church. The Bible itself is not immune from this partial and thus distorted vision. We come to see that a generation of remembering and rearticulating theology is needed, in which the feminine dimension of the Church must be recovered.

During that retreat we did a tiny experiment of rearticulation. We went through the familiar hymn "Praise to the Lord," noting all the masculine terms that refer to God, substituting for them feminine terms. We then sang the hymn using the feminine terms. It went like this:

Praise to the Lady, the almighty, the Queen of creation!
Oh my soul, praise her, for she is thy health and salvation!
All ye who hear, now to her temple draw near;
Join me in glad adoration!

Praise to the Lady, who o'er all things so wondrously
   reigneth,
Shieldeth thee under her wings, yea, so gently sustaineth!
Hast thou not seen how thy desires e'er have been
Granted in what she ordaineth?

Praise to the Lady, who doth prosper thy work and defend
   thee;
Surely her goodness and mercy here daily attend thee
Ponder anew what the Almighty can do,
If with her love she befriend thee.

We then shared our feelings about singing the hymn
this way. A man spoke up quickly and with agitation. "It
offended me. The masculine terms in the original hymn
are meant to cover all humanity. Why play these language
games?" Then a woman spoke with quiet grace and
strength. "It felt wonderful to sing praise to God who is
also feminine as I am, whose humanity is my humanity,
and in whose divinity I as a woman share fully." Two
positions 180 degrees apart. Our emotional feelings run
deep in the liturgy and hymnology on which we have
been nourished all our lives. We will need to be gentle
with one another as we review and rewrite the language of
creed, prayer, and hymn. It is amazing how thoroughly
masculine is the language of the worship of the Church! It
is promising as well as threatening to anticipate the
transformation of prayer and worship that will come
through recovery of the feminine dimension of the
Church.

One sign of that recovery already powerfully
happening in the Church is the increasing numbers of
clergywomen. I was listening to a woman preach during a
recent Kirkridge workshop on preaching. She preached
with a clear grace and eloquent simplicity. I was much

taken with her and her sermon. I found myself unusually open to the word of God through her preaching. Allowing for and sorting out all the vibes resonating in me, I realized how impoverished the worship of the Church has been over the centuries to have had sermons preached almost exclusively by men. Not just that women have been deprived of exercising the priestly and preaching roles, but that both men and women have been deprived of the nurture, prophecy, and insight which are now coming into the life of the Church through the distinct and differentiated women's experience. Just as the inclusion of blacks in our society does not mean a loss or put-down for whites, but rather an enrichment of our common humanity, so the ministry of clergywomen in the Church will transform our worship of God, calling men and women alike into the one spiritual body.

A few months ago I sat in on a retreat for women who were exploring the theology and psychology of their being women of faith. One of the two leaders, both of whom were women and one of whom was ordained, reminded us that two of the most powerful role models for women in the Bible are Eve and Mary. Scheming, seductive, manipulative, betraying Eve! and the virgin Mary! The leader said, "What role models! Most of us can't fully identify with either, and don't fit comfortably into either role." She sparked our imagination in searching the scriptures and the history of the Church for feminine role models. She pointed out that the Bible speaks typically and primarily of "men's" sins: pride, lust, aggressiveness, and noted that the Bible does not feature "women's" sins: manipulativeness, passivity, helplessness, dependency, jealousy. She helped us realize anew that women in our culture are guilty of undervaluing themselves, undercutting other women, and being less than they are called to be. I watched women hearken to the notion that they were of as much value in the eyes of God as men, that their calling was just as important as that of men, that they could help to bring about the transformation of the life and ministry of the Church. The retreat concluded with the sharing of communion, led by the leader who was a clergywoman. There had been talk about references in the Bible and in the Church to women's "uncleanness," blood, menstruation, pregnancy. Reference had been made to the discomfort some men have expressed in receiving communion from a pregnant or menstruating woman. (Oh, the ostracism, repugnance, and belittling that men and often women have visited upon women in the Church! As though only men could be holy in the priestly role.) I watched and participated as these women received the sacramental elements from their sister. Tears flowed, faces shone, hands joined, hearts were lifted up with joy as the Spirit moved in our midst, giving us all power to conceive. Sarah must have been smiling! (And Abraham too, I trust. It is possible isn't it to be liberated retroactively? People like me have to hope so!) Being reborn comes by recovering the feminine dimension of the Church.

Being reborn comes by recovering the feminine dimension of culture. Sarah has been active in our society in recent years, and it is time—Abraham has run things long enough. It's amazing to reflect that women in America received the power to vote only fifty years ago. Presently in the Congress, out of more than 400 representatives only a handful are women, and of the 100 senators, only one is a woman. But the Women's Movement is gathering strength, and we will all be better off when there is full equality and representation of citizenship, equal pay for equal work, and so on.

I have three daughters. Although each may hope for marriage and children, all are developing careers outside the home to have the opportunity and option of supporting themselves financially and pursuing their own dreams. Only as women break out of dependence upon men and gather their own responsible strength will a healthy interdependence of men and women be possible. Commenting about the Total Woman philosophy articulated by Marabel Morgan, Gail Sheehy, the author of *Passages*, wrote, "If there is anything 'total' about adhering to these principles, it would be total personal dishonesty. The woman is never told to do or say what she feels or believes, only what she thinks will bring her safety and fabulous kisses and improved kitchen appliances. It insults a man's intelligence and it trains a woman to remain a manipulative child. That may work acceptably for the first half of life. But playacting bodes ill for any truth knowing, and people must be willing to know their own truth if they are to pass into midlife as adults."[7]

Our society is being reborn as women take their appropriate roles in defining and shaping it. The energy of transformation is coming from the recovery of the feminine. Such change may at first be threatening to many men and women whose security is lodged in the traditional way. But life will be more human and more fulfilling when it becomes more cooperative, warmer, intuitive, and sensitive, when "being" as well as "doing"

[7] Gail Sheehy, *Passages* (New York: Dutton, 1976), p. 208.

is encouraged for both men and women. At the turn of the century Rilke foresaw what was coming when he wrote:

> Women, in whom life lingers and dwells more immediately, more fruitfully and more confidently, must surely have become fundamentally riper people, more human people, than easygoing man, who is not pulled down below the surface of life by the weight of any fruit of his body, and who, presumptuous and hasty, undervalues what he thinks he loves. This humanity of woman, borne its full time in suffering and humiliation, will come to light when she will have stripped off the conventions of mere feminity in the mutations of her outward status, and those men who do not yet feel it approaching today will be surprised and struck by it. . . . Some day there will be . . . women whose name will no longer signify merely an opposite of the masculine, but something in itself, something that makes one think, not of any complement and limit, but only of life and existence: the feminine human being. This advance will (at first much against the will of the outstripped men) change the love-experience, which is now full of error, will alter it from the ground up, reshape it into a relation that is meant to be of one human being to another, no longer of man to woman. And this more human love (that will fulfill itself, infinitely considerate and gentle, and kind and clear in binding and releasing) will resemble that which we are preparing with struggle and toil, the love that consists in this, that two solitudes protect and border and salute each other.[8]

We are reborn, with Sarah, when we recover the feminine dimension of God, ourselves, the Church, and

---

[8] Rainer Maria Rilke, *Letters to a Young Poet*, trans. M.D. Herter Norton, pp. 58–59.

society. *And,* with Sarah, such a transformation often comes to us when we are "past the age" . . . old or getting older. So to our second major affirmation:

Rebirth happens to us when we are old. What is old? Why is it that when we get older, we are especially vulnerable to being reborn? How are we reborn when we are old? (John 3:4). We wouldn't want to put age restrictions on the movements of the Spirit who turns our heart-sighs into songs and blows over our fences of fear. After all, it appears that Abraham and Sarah were in their seventies, Jeremiah was a youth when God called him, and so forth. The Spirit is no respecter of chronological age with regard to persons and institutions ready for rebirth.

And yet, the more we learn about the process of adult development, the more we realize that people often experience significant rebirth during the middle years. Middle age extends from the mid-thirties into the sixties, and many of us begin to take stock of where we've been and where we're going at some point in those years. We've lived long enough to have some of our dreams come true, some partially fulfilled, others turn into nightmares, and still others die. We know we need to revise our dreams or dream new ones. There comes a high noon moment or turning point when we can see both horizons and, like Tevye in *Fiddler on the Roof,* begin to sing of sunrise and sunset. We begin to mark our lives no longer from our birth but now from our death.

Awareness of our own death is critical to the possibility of being reborn. Such awareness may come in the realization that some roles and relationships are dying or obsolete, that we are living in tents again and it is time to move on into new roles. Or it may come in the realization that we don't have forever anymore, that some values and doctrines have proven false or transitory, and that once again it is time to evaluate our values. As the stable order of our lives is loosened internally or externally, we are nudged or thrown onto the road again. Awareness of our own death opens up a new transition time that can become transformation time.

Our experience of being reborn varies. A recent article was titled "Born Again Conversions Are on the Rise Among The Mature." The article starts,

> Bob Ash, a burly, mustachioed 50-year-old salesman, stood recently with the congregation of St. Paul's Episcopal church here, his palms upraised and extended, quietly joining in singing "alleluia, alleluia." The service was being held in the auditorium of Darien High School because the parish has attracted so many like Mr. Ash that the present sanctuary is too small. With an enrollment six times what it was five years ago, numbering 1200 at present, parish spokesmen say it is the most heavily attended Episcopal church in the country. Mr. Ash is typical of those who are drawn by the charismatic character of the church. . . . He is also illustrative of the tendency within current revivalistic "Jesus movements" to attract older people. . . . Most experts believe that conversion is not usually the result of a visible or catastrophic crisis for most born again Christians. It is more often found to be the culmination of an inchoate inner restlessness and dissatisfaction with life.[9]

Whether we stagnate or experience rebirth has to do with how we face our inner restlessness, discontents and fears.

Andrzej Wajda, the fifty-one-year-old Polish filmmaker, expresses his rebirth somewhat differently from Bob Ash. Discussing with a reporter his growth as a director, Wajda

---

[9]*The New York Times*, Dec. 1, 1977, p. 41.

said, "As I am getting older, I am going from dark to light, to things that are joyful. Age gives me the right. When I was very young, I was thinking about how awful it is to get old. But youth has incredible weaknesses—being afriad of sex, school, of life in general. Age has its advantages. One is not afraid anymore."[10]

When our own aging forces us to face death in ourselves and others, we discover our spirit is not defeated. We respect death but no longer fear it. We cease being ashamed of our tears or our joys. We affirm publicly what we believe privately. If we want to wear one green sock and one yellow one we do, regardless of what "they" think. We recapture the initiative of our own lives. It is like beginning again under our own authority.

"The Santa Fe Experience"[11] describes radical career changes made by people in their middle years, for whom rebirth required profound changes of geography, profession, life style, roles, and self-definition. These people moved from a variety of places and professions to Santa Fe, where the ambience appeared to facilitate the discovery and shaping of a new and simple life style. These men and women were seeking autonomy, freedom from the constraint of usual work scenes, the courage to confront their lives in solitude, and to find and honor the kernel of their own being. They determined to integrate their work with their life. Their rebirth dramatizes the vision faced by many whose choices are not so radical but who also are trying to begin again under their own authority.

When we realize we are getting older we discover we

---

[10] "A Polish 'Baby Doll' Opens at Yale," *The New York Times*, Apr. 15, 1977, p. C3.

[11] Seymour B. Sarason, *Work, Aging and Social Change* (New York: Macmillan, 1977), p. 165.

have power to begin again. Elie Wiesel wrote, "When He created man, God gave him a secret—and that secret was not how to begin, but how to begin again. . . . It is not given to man to begin; that privilege is God's alone. But it is given to man to begin again—and he does so every time he chooses to defy death and side with the living."[12] Biblical rebirth is always a time and place of beginning again, a time of letting go yesterday's fears and embracing today's hopes, a time of letting the dead bury their dead (Luke 9:60) while we go to proclaim the New Age.

Beginning again means going on the road again. At a Midlife Journey Workshop at Kirkridge a thirty-eight-year-old woman named Chris wrote a little story on the theme *Alice Doesn't Live Here Anymore*. She wrote, "Alice doesn't live here anymore. She left, and someone else has moved in. The new woman is something different from Alice! What a pleasant change! Alice kept the shades drawn, the door locked, and was always crabby to her neighbors. She must have been a lonely and unhappy person! But the new tenant—Wow! Warm and alive, windows and doors always open, garden in bloom, and the teakettle on the stove. She's really human—joys and hurts, too, but she seems ready to meet them and deal with them. I'm sure glad to know her. Poor Alice—wonder where she's gone. I don't really care—I'm just glad!"

At the end of the workshop we gave Chris the gift of a new name: Chris-Alice (Chrysalis), to identify and affirm her new birth. Chris-Alice doesn't live here anymore. She is going from darkness to light. She isn't afraid any longer. She is being reborn.

Bob-Abraham doesn't live here anymore. I am being

---

[12] Elie Wiesel, *Messengers of God* (New York: Random House, 1976), p. 32.

reborn. However old you are, and especially if you are "past the age," you can be reborn. T. S. Eliot reminds us that old men and women are called to be explorers. All of us: Sarahs, Abrahams, Bob Ashes, Andrzej Wajdas, and Chris-Alices are ripe for rebirth as we experience our aging and dying. Rebirth comes out of awareness of death, and strangely, when we realize that we are *old*, we may freshly discover that we are *young!*

It is when we are "past the age" that we may enter into a new childhood of the Spirit. I do *not* mean child*ish*ness but the child*like*ness of which Jesus spoke when he said, ". . . unless you turn and become like children, you will never enter the kingdom of heaven" (Matthew 18:3). Paul Ricoeur speaks of such childlikeness as a "second naïvete," beyond our first innocence, and beyond the skepticism of our first wisdom, in a deeper wisdom that yields childlike wonderment and humility. King Lear came to himself in his second naïvete, when he was "past the age," when he saw himself and his three daughters as they really were. He speaks to Cordelia in the time of their dying as though it were the time of their living for the first time:

> Come, let's away to prison;
> we too alone will sing like birds i' the cage.
> When thou dost ask me blessing,
> I'll kneel down and ask of thee forgiveness.
> So we'll live and pray and sing,
> and tell old tales and laugh at gilded butterflies,
> and hear poor rogues talk of court news;
> and we'll talk with them too,
> who loses and who wins;
> who's in, who's out,
> and take upon 's the mystery of things,
> as if we were God's spies.[13]

---

[13] William Shakespeare, *King Lear*, act V, scene 3.

Lo, I tell you a mystery, but the mystery is larger than any telling. The mystery was made known through a child. The mystery becomes known again and again to us when we become like children.

When we are old-and-young-again we may find enough humility to ask our children for their forgiveness and enough magnanimity to forgive our own parents for their mistakes with us. We may give ourselves permission to play and pray and laugh a bit at the buzz about who's in and who's out in the competitions of the day. We may give ourselves permission to feed birds and fondle plants, read books and listen to music, dance and take hikes without feeling guilty about not being productive. We may discover that it is time and that we are ready to grow the life of the Spirit, to bear the inner fruit which satisfies.

When we are old-and-young-again, we may believe once more in angels. In his article "When Religion Cast Off Wonder, Hollywood Seized It," Andrew Greeley wrote,

Who are the flying saucer type aliens who appear amid profound, prolonged and very loud fanfare at the end of [the movie] "Close Encounters Of The Third Kind?" What sort of creature is it who is benign, has a dazzlingly brilliant intellect, loves cute little kids and opens its arms in Christ-like greeting? The type of being who appears in blinding light, likes to touch down on remote mountain tops, communicates in musical harmonies against harp and organ background and is childlike in appearance? Who are they? Angels, that's who. [Greeley affirms the religious quality of the movie that declares "we are not alone" as a kind of companion-piece to the Star Wars benediction "May the Force be with you." He says that] The replacement of the Bible by science fiction as a source of Wonder is not an accident. . . . When angels in the marvel-filled scriptures go out the front door, alien beings and science fiction come in the back door along with astrology, witchcraft, tarot cards, gods in flaming chariots and a lot of other pre-Biblical superstitions. You can demythologize Wonder out of your sacred books but you can't demythologize the hunger for the wonderful out of the human personality. . . .[14]

We get attacks of hunger for the wonderful when we are old-and-young-again. Our hearts yearn beyond what seems possible toward the place where all things are possible for those who believe, those who hope, those who love, those who are like little children. Beasts and angels attended that birth in Bethlehem and ministered to Jesus in the desert when he was being tempted by Satan to adopt yesterday's will of God. Beasts and angels also attend us when we are being reborn. The natural and the spiritual. Earth and heaven. Angels are bringers and singers of good news, new beginnings, forgivings, healings, and hopings. Angels represent the creative energies that promise to deliver and delight us. When we are in the process of being reborn, we are freshly receptive to marvelous energies and like children regain the capacity of rapture.

But there are also demons. Rilke once wrote, "If my devils are to leave me, I am afraid my angels will take flight as well." We can't be vulnerable to the one without the other. Demons represent those chaotic energies that threaten to destroy us. When we are in process of being reborn we are vulnerable once again to destructive energies, and, like children, we have to learn again how to cope with terrible powers.

Bruno Bettelheim, in his book *The Uses of Enchantment*, shows us how fairy tales provide fantasy material for the

---

[14] Andrew Greeley, "When Religion Cast Off Wonder, Hollywood Seized It," *The New York Times*, Nov. 27, 1977, sec. 2, p. 1.

child to play his fears and hopes against in ways that are safe and enable the child's development toward maturity. In the story of "The Three Little Pigs," "the houses the pigs build are symbolic of man's progress in history: from a lean-to shack to a wooden house, finally to a house of solid brick"[15] that is strong enough to withstand the huffing and puffing of the big bad wolf. The fairy tale teaches that one must plan intelligently to protect one's self against the wolf, which represents those forces within us and outside that can destroy us. The third pig, the oldest and wisest, "is even able to predict correctly the behavior of the wolf—the enemy, or stranger within, which tries to seduce and trap us; and therefore the third pig is able to defeat powers both stronger and more ferocious than he is. The wild and destructive wolf stands for all asocial, unconscious, devouring powers against which one must learn to protect one's self, and which one can defeat through the strength of one's ego."[16]

We can literally incorporate the destructive powers threatening us into our own bodies, just as the third pig ate the wolf. We need to recover in our second naïvete the capacity of a child to imagine the chaos within and without that threatens us, to let it loose in our imagination, in the knowledge that it represents an important part of ourselves—our most powerful energies—and that by our intelligence these awe-ful powers can be outwitted, made to serve our own purposes, and thus to expand our selves and our lives.

Nietzsche wrote, "chaos, trusted, becomes a dancing star." A beautiful image to suggest that, like children, we

---

[15] Bruno Bettelheim, *The Uses of Enchantment*, p. 42.
[16] *Ibid.*, p. 42.

can entertain chaotic powers and indeed embrace them, not to become like them or to be destroyed by them, but to integrate them into our own self-system. It is when the lion (violent energy) and the lamb (gentle energy) lie down together in us that we become whole. We need both our angels and our demons to receive and achieve full integrity. This leads us to the third affirmation of this chapter, which is:

Rebirth Yields Integrity of the Self. We struggle toward an inward rebirth of the self, an integration of the estranged or unarticulated parts of the self (for me: anger, grief, sexuality), in which the shadow side is embraced and the personality is rounded out, contributing to the formation of a more whole self. Such rebirth may express itself in movement from a negative behavior pattern such as alcoholism to a positive pattern of sobriety. That is, the change may be ethical in character and exhibit visible behavioral effects. But the more fundamental change is ontological, involving an alteration of one's basic attitude, values, orientation, and faith-commitment. Such a change takes place inwardly and may not be immediately visible in outer behavior. For example, Nicodemus was already a good man in religious and moral terms, and yet he still needed to be reborn. He needed to have his life recentered in God.

Being recentered in God is a painful business. I feel as if I am being born into a new integrity out of the wounds, disruptions, and sorrows of my life, as God gently collects the fragmented parts of me and molds me into a more whole and focused person. Broken and disheveled as my recent life has been, it is permeated by grace and I am forgivable. I am being led, as we all are being led, toward

Shalem,[17] a spiritual maturity that does not consist in static moral perfection but is a dynamic process unfolding toward fulfillment or completion (Matthew 5:48).

One of my favorite images of this integrity was provided by Theodore Roethke:

> Near this rose, in this grove of sun-parched, wind-warped
> madronas,
> Among the half-dead trees, I came upon the true ease of
> myself,
> As if another man appeared out of the depths of my being,
> And I stood outside myself,
> Beyond becoming and perishing,
> A something wholly other,
> As if I swayed out on the wildest wave alive,
> And yet was still.
> And I rejoiced in being what I was. . . .[18]

I am being reborn as I come upon "the true ease of myself," when all the wild in me and the stillness abide together: when the lion and lamb, the prodigal and elder son, Mary and Martha, Sindbad the Seaman and Sindbad the Porter, the sheep and the wolf come together in strong peace. I come upon my true ease when I am able to live in my own skin, when I'm comfortable in my roles and relationships, when there is a good fit between my self and my self-image, my sense of vocation and my actual job, my values and my actual life style, when there is integration

---

[17] The Shalem concept is explored by Tilden Edwards in his monograph *Spiritual Growth: An Empirical Exploration of Its Meaning, Sources and Implications* (Washington, D.C.: Metropolitan Ecumenical Training Center, Inc., 1974).

[18] Theodore Roethke, "The Rose," in *The Collected Poems of Theodore Roethke*, p. 199.

of my self in my world. It is as though all the multiple selves in me fit together in one whole self.

Morris West describes the kind of congruence toward which we all struggle in another image: "Yesterday I met a whole man. It is a rare experience, but always an illuminating and ennobling one. It costs so much to be a full human being that there are very few who have the enlightenment, or the courage, to pay the price. . . . One has to abandon altogether the search for security, and reach out to the risk of living with both arms. One has to embrace the world like a lover, and yet demand no easy return of love. One has to accept pain as a condition of existence. One has to court doubt and darkness as the cost of knowing. One needs a will stubborn in conflict, but apt always to the total acceptance of every consequence of living and dying."[19]

A person becoming whole lives in a tent. One has no way of bottling or preserving such wholeness. There is always the pain, the uneasy movement of the wild and the still in us, one or the other taking advantage, always the risking of what security one has, the battle for balance between strength and sensitivity, discipline and serendipity, steel will and supple spirit.

There is a continuing need to love the stranger-shadow parts of the self, the underdeveloped parts that constantly clamor for attention to be paid. The Spirit whispers or roars to us in the ugly or unacceptable parts of our lives, calling us to embrace that disorder which is here to stay and to wrestle it to a painful blessing. It is as though the competing, conflicting selves in us struggle for ascendancy

---

[19] Morris L. West, *The Shoes of the Fisherman* (New York: Morrow, 1963), p. 254.

or for psychosynthesis, as the three brothers in *The Brothers Karamazov* contend: Ivan the cool skeptic, Alyosha the gentle mystic, Dmitri the passionate lover. I consider that in recent years the Dmitri in me has fought his way to parity with my Ivan and Alyosha, grounding and humanizing and upsetting both! Dmitri has made me more real, less nice, more earthy, less polite.

One of our needs in the process of rebirth is to believe that our total life story is somehow acceptable to God, within his purpose. We long to taste those moments in which we know our sins are not unpardonable and that we are held in hands which are gentle and strong. The hands of one who loves us without condition or ending. When we are granted to live in such an abiding faith, we may be able to feel in our bones the kind of integrity of which Erik Erikson wrote: "Integrity . . . is the acceptance of one's one and only life cycle and of the people who have become significant to it as something that had to be and that by necessity permitted of no substitutions. It thus means a new different love of one's parents, free of the wish that they should have been different, and an acceptance of the fact that one's life is one's own responsibility."[20]

This integrity is a kind of providence in retrospect, a looking back in faith that allows a looking forward in hope. It consists in receiving the gift and task of one's selfhood and using one's power to conceive new life. It is to become like a tree planted by streams of water, yielding its fruit in its season (Psalms 1:3). It is to be in accord with the season of one's life, to move in one's natural rhythm,

---

[20] Erik H. Erikson, "Identity and the Life Cycle," *Psychological Issues,* vol. I, no. 1 (1959), p. 98.

to resonate with one's own inner music. But more, it is to participate as a person of integrity in the rebirth of one's society. This leads us to the fourth affirmation of this chapter:

Rebirth yields integrity of the nation. A biblical understanding of rebirth calls not only for the integrity of the self but the integrity of the nation. Just as the estranged parts of the self are to be integrated into the transformed self, so the estranged people of the nation are to be included in the transformed nation. And indeed the estranged nations of the world are to be included in the great commonwealth of Yahweh. Private integrity and public integrity go together; one cannot exist without the other. We can even say that *only* those who are engaged with the persons, institutions, and environment of their time and place seeking *public* rebirth are in the process of being reborn personally. Isaiah gives us a vision of this communal or national integrity:

> I exult for joy in Yahweh,
> my soul rejoices in my God,
> for he has clothed me in the garments of salvation,
> he has wrapped me in the cloak of *integrity*,
> like a bridegroom wearing his wreath,
> like a bride adorned in her jewels.

> For as the earth makes fresh things grow,
> as a garden makes seeds spring up,
> so will the Lord Yahweh make both *integrity* and praise
> spring up in the sight of the nations.

> About Zion I will not be silent,
> about Jerusalem I will not grow weary,
> until her *integrity* shines out like the dawn
> and her salvation flames like a torch.

The nations then will see your *integrity*,
all the kings your glory,
and you will be called by a new name,
one which the mouth of Yahweh will confer.

You are to be a crown of splendor in the hand of Yahweh,
a princely diadem in the hand of your God;
no longer are you to be named "Forsaken,"
nor your land "Abandoned,"
but you shall be called "My Delight,"
and your land "The Wedded,"
for Yahweh takes delight in you
and your land will have its wedding.

Isaiah 61:10–62:4, JB (italics added)

Isaiah ranges in soaring hope from the integrity of the self—"he has wrapped *me* in the cloak of integrity"—to the integrity of God's special people—"About *Zion* I will not be silent . . . until *her* integrity shines out like the dawn." With Paul we can carry the vision further and imagine the whole creation (Romans 8:22) yearning toward the day when everything in the cosmos will shine in the Spirit (Colossians 1:10).

What does such a vast and glorious vision mean for you and me? It means that for biblical people there is no place to hide. There is no way to hug our new birth to ourselves, for an indigenous part of our new name and calling is to work for human liberation. The purpose of rebirth is not private escape but public responsibility. We are not reborn to tune out of the needs of the world via the route of detachment espoused in some Eastern religions, or in churches for which the salvation of the soul is enough, or in some human potential systems where the functioning adjustment of the psyche is the goal. The purpose of biblical rebirth is always *for the sake of* the neighbor, the other, the prisoner, the hungry, the sick, the least of these (Matthew 25:31 ff.).

God called Moses, not to conduct prayer groups, but to lead a rebellion against the political tyranny of his time and place (Exodus 3). Moses was afraid and didn't want to do it. But he did. Look afresh at the Magnificat, which we so often shroud in angelic Christmas music, muffling if not stifling the hard imperatives of its charter.

> My soul proclaims the greatness of the Lord
> and my spirit exults in God my savior;
> because he has looked upon his lowly handmaid.
> Yes, from this day forward all generations will call me
> blessed,
> for the Almighty has done great things for me.
> Holy is his name,
> and his mercy reaches from age to age for those who fear
> him.
> He has shown the power of his arm,
> he has routed the proud of heart.
> He has pulled down princes from their thrones and exalted
> the lowly.
> The hungry he has filled with good things, the rich sent
> empty away.
> He has come to the help of Israel, his servant, mindful of his
> mercy
> —according to the promise he made to our ancestors—
> of his mercy to Abraham and to his descendants for ever.
>
> *Luke 1: 46–55*, JB

Mary directs us to the social revolution the Lord of history is bringing about in Jesus! God called Jesus, not to be a pastoral patsy of the rich, nor a private chaplain to the White Houses of his day, but to:

preach good news to the poor . . .
proclaim release to the captives
and recovering of sight to the blind,
to set at liberty those who are oppressed. . . .

Luke 4:18

Jesus was not well received that day in his hometown
synagogue. In fact, they tried to kill him, so offended were
they by his message of human liberation. Like the people
in that synagogue, we're often offended by the call to
liberate the oppressed and would prefer to rest in our
private piety. Like Moses and Mary we're afraid of getting
involved in the messy, dangerous business of confronting
the powerful and lifting up the poor. We'd rather protect
what we've got and not put our security to risk. But we
have to choose. We can't be reborn only privately. The
Bible knows nothing of such an event. The only kind of
rebirth the Bible finds credible and creditable is that which
yields both integrity of the self and of the nation.
Christians are among those called to embody such dual
integrity. Each of us must find ways in our own journeys
and responsibilities to be about such ministries of human
liberation. In the next chapter, I'll describe some ways we
are seeking such integrity in our work at Kirkridge.

5 | Going Home

These all died in faith, not having received what was
promised, but having seen it and greeted it from afar,
and having acknowledged that they were strangers
and exiles on the earth. For people who speak thus
make it clear that they are seeking a homeland. If
they had been thinking of that land from which they
had gone out, they would have had opportunity to
return. But as it is, they desire a better country, that is,
a heavenly one. Therefore God is not ashamed to be
called their God, for he has prepared for them a city.
Hebrews 11:13–16

*A*BRAHAM and Sarah never made it to the promised land. They spent their lives making it. They were journeyers all the way. They had tastes, glimpses, revelations of the promising land, their real home, but they never arrived. They kept on living in tents and being reborn. They might have gone back, but they chose to go ahead, looking for home in the future. They accepted the fact that they were strangers and exiles on the earth, pilgrims and outsiders. The promise kept sounding in their hearts. So they kept on going home with their people.

We are going home with our people. We who have left home know that we will never again be at home on this earth. We mourn the loss of our home-world, we acknowledge that we are displaced persons and that we will never be "home safe." Yet, the homing hope draws and drives us on the way. We believe that our true home is out there, ahead, and that Abraham and Sarah and all their companions are our fellow travelers. We're going home with them.

How did we ever get mixed up with such a strange crowd? Are these people really *our* people? It's like waking up and hanging out of an upstairs window in a Breughel painting. Look at those crazy people down there: washing clothes, fighting in the alley, making love behind the barn, skating, urinating on trees, smoking pipes, playing cards. *These* are our people. *They* are going home with us. We are not a neat, tidy sober congregation seated side by side in back-to-back pews facing forward. We are a milling crowd, pushing, shoving, loving, laughing—a Moses-mob in the wilderness on our way. We are not the righteous, but the sinners whom Christ came to call. We're the common people who still hear Jesus gladly. Because we have left home and live in tents and know what it is to be outsiders, because our lives have been broken and we have been shedding tears and roles, we can recognize others who are wounded, searching, vulnerable. We discover one another as brothers and sisters in a new and expanding family, on the way home. The journey brought us together. The quest made us fellow pilgrims, kinfolk.

> Befell that in that season, on a day
> In Southwark at the Tabard, as I lay
> Ready upon my pilgrimage to start
> To Canterbury with a pious heart,
> At night there came into that hostelry
> Full nine and twenty in a company
> Of Sundry folk, by chance together there
> In fellowship; and pilgrims too, they were
> That on to Canterbury meant to ride.[1]

---

[1] Geoffrey Chaucer, "Prologue to The Canterbury Tales," lines 19–27, *Adventures in English Literature*, ed. J. B. Priestley and Josephine Spear (New York: Harcourt Brace Jovanovich, 1963), p. 70.

Like Chaucer's pilgrims we are, by divine chance, together in fellowship. Because we need hospitality, being strangers on our way, we understand that other stranger-pilgrims need welcome. In fact, hospitality to strangers is our thing (Hebrews 13:1-2)! That's another part of what the journey's all about: to gather other outsiders of the human family together with us and to head for the homecoming banquet in our father/mother's house (Luke 15:22-24). We're going home!

And on the way we take time to tell tall tales and share the stories of our lives, listening for news.

> Shall all wanderers over the earth, all homeless ones,
> All against whom doors are shut and words spoken—
> Shall these find the earth less strange tonight?
> Shall they hear news, a whisper on the night wind?[2]

Whispered good news sounds sweetest to homeless wanderers who strain to hear a familiar welcome.

Acts 2 tells us that there were people from "every nation under heaven" gathered on the first Pentecost, all of whom heard the Spirit speaking to them in their own language. This suggests that all our provisional homeland places here are authentic signposts of the real homeland to the extent that they are Spirit-inclusive, hospitable to outsiders. Then in Acts 10 we watch the Spirit falling on outsiders, astounding Peter and others who were sure the Spirit was for insiders only (in that setting, the Jews). But here was the Spirit (no respecter of personal or institutional exclusion) doing the unthinkable: falling upon Gentiles! A paradigm of the surprising Spirit who

---

[2] Carl Sandburg, "Special Starlight," *Complete Poems of Carl Sandburg* (New York: Harcourt Brace Jovanovich, 1950).

continues to fall on outsiders every where and every time. As soon as we draw lines to keep people out, we can be sure the Spirit is already crossing those lines and moving in the hearts of those whom we have defined out, in an ever-widening circle of love. There is no nation, no person outside the reach of the Spirit. It is a fundamental characteristic of the Spirit that she falls on outsiders as well as insiders. A sign of the future, of tomorrow's will of God, is to be seen wherever outsiders are being welcomed and boundaries of exclusion crossed.

Often it seems that outsiders are primary spokespeople for the Spirit. If we want to see the frontiers of human inclusion where the Spirit is calling us to cross boundaries and to make invitations, we must identify in our churches and communities those situations where people are being excluded. If we would participate in the hospitality work of the Spirit, we must take responsibility for opening up those frontiers near us, where we live, work, vote, and play. That is the way in which we create the future and allow the future to take shape in us and in our community. That is what we do when we are going home with our people.

Kirkridge is the place where I have been going home with my people in recent years. Kirkridge was founded in 1942 by John Oliver Nelson, a Presbyterian minister. He was inspired by the Iona Community in Scotland, where there has been a Celtic form of Christianity dating back to A.D. 600. He wanted to establish a similar place in this country, where concern for the renewal of Church and world might be located and embodied. In 1942 Nelson bought a farmhouse with 350 acres of land near Bangor, in northeastern Pennsylvania. A few friends joined with him in the early days of visioning, and the dream took its initial form. Much physical work was done in those first years to restore the central room of the farmhouse, built in 1815, and to develop a lodge on top of the mountainside.

I first touched this land in the winter of 1947; I was one of fifteen college students who came from Yale for a weekend retreat. We all talked, shared the experience of silence and Bible study, worked on the building and land, opened our hearts to one another on the mission of the Church. It was my first retreat, and I was profoundly moved. I was to come back many times in the years that followed, until I "came home" in 1974 as the director of Kirkridge, succeeding John Nelson.

What is Kirkridge? From the beginning its special code phrase has been: Picket and Pray. Concern for commitment to both the outward and the inward journey and an appropriate balance of the two. If we are engaged in "picketing"—social activist work for racial, gender, sexual, political, economic, religious justice in the world, and peace among the nations—without prayer, our work may lack spiritual rootage, depth, stamina. We may lack awareness of our own sin and partial vision, strength of faith to witness in patient endurance without the need for immediate results to validate our action.

If, on the other hand, we are engaged in "praying"— spiritual development, personal healing, growth toward integration of the self in meditation, intentional seeking of union with and love of God—without picketing, our praying may be superficial, uncostly, privatist. We may lack compassionate/courageous confrontation with evil in the structures of the world and pursue a disembodied spirituality that does not lead to human transformation.

Full-bodied Christianity calls for incarnation, words
becoming enfleshed in deeds, love of God and neighbor,
energized by persons graced with a healthy love of self.

Kirkridge has intended to be and become such a people,
place, and power since 1942. Its "incarnations" over the
years have changed according to changing social context,
leadership of staff and Board, constituency, resources. In
1978 the Board developed a fresh statement of
indentity/vocation:

> K i r k r i d g e is a center
> rooted in Christ
> where people on pilgrimage
> seek community
> in the midst of diversity
> and experience
> the transforming power of the Spirit
> for personal wholeness
> reconciliation
> justice in the world.

The abiding Kirkridge symbol, a Celtic cross, embodies in
its thrusting crossbeams the masculine dimensions of focus,
clarity, direction, decision, intention, and its circle
expresses the feminine dimensions of healing, integration,
union, wholeness. Leaving home and going home resonate
in creative polarity in that rich symbol whose fresh
meanings and images yield self-renewing energies in our
day.

The current Kirkridge program includes events
reflecting both picket and pray concerns. Though we can
handle up to 100 persons for a single event in our five
facilities, our more characteristic event consists of fifteen to
twenty people living, eating, sleeping, and talking
together around a single issue in one facility. On a given

weekend we might have a group Growing the Life of the Spirit in one facility, persons engaged in The Art of Healing in another facility, others working on Praying and Peace-making in a third facility, and others exploring Simple Living in yet another facility.

An enduring Kirkridge concern is to provide special sanctuary and encouragement to persons and groups outside the mainstream of society. Persons and groups oppressed, forgotten, scapegoated, deprived economically or socially. Kirkridge itself is an "outsider" institution in that it exists outside, though alongside, the established Church. It maintains an ongoing lover's quarrel with the Church, acknowledging common heritage and hope, but ever seeking to call the Church out of its cultural bondage to be a vanguard of the future instead of a rearguard. Full of failure, sin, and pride ourselves, we who identify with Kirkridge nevertheless want to be an outpost of the people of God in this world, providing special welcome to "strangers," "the least of these," outsiders. Although most of our events are filled with insiders, some of our projects are aimed at particular outsider groups. Let me describe four such groups for whom we have been concerned in recent years, people who are economic, sexual, familial, or political outsiders in our time.

Here are four pictures in our human family album where the Spirit is calling us to create new futures. (There are many other album pages we could ponder—as many pages as there are special categories of human need, suffering, hope.) Picture a bunch of people sitting around the huge stone fireplace at the Kirkridge Farmhouse. How did these people get to this hearth? Jane Nelson, then Associate Director of Kirkridge, had a concern that we find a way of extending hospitality to people suffering unemployment. Bill Cohea, a neighbor and friend, got the idea of putting an ad in the papers. So a tiny ad appeared in the Sunday *New York Times*, November 21, 1976:

WANTED: UNEMPLOYED MEN AND WOMEN...
concerned to look at goals and values in time of transition. Kirkridge Retreat and Study Center offers you a gift of three free days in the country. Write or call....

Monday morning the calls began to come, from Queens, Manhattan, Brooklyn, Connecticut, New Jersey, New York, Pennsylvania. "What's Kirkridge.... What's the hitch?" We explained there was no hitch; we just wanted to offer breathing space to people suffering unemployment and a chance to evaluate life styles, roles, relationships in a context of quiet and community.

Late Wednesday afternoon, December 1, people began to arrive at the farmhouse: wary, weary, and curious. Sitting round the hearth that evening we began to hear and see one another: a woman in her fifties, free-lance writer, articulate, perceptive, searching; an investment broker at mid-forties, out of work a year and a half, desperate intensity, severe family tensions; an art teacher about forty, divorced, ripped off by her lawyer, three children, tough, hurt, gentled by enduring; a sixty-year-old sheet metal worker, an easygoing, smiling, flannel-shirted man; a fifty-four-year-old corporate executive asking, "Do I want to get back into the corporate crunch ... if I can?"; a fifty-one-year-old woman, moxie, learned how to survive, wide knowledge of resources, how to live on the cheap. Twenty-one of us in all: Jews, Catholics, Protestants. I said to them, "Kirkridge has made a small investment in you, but you are a gutsy group of people to spot a tiny ad in a newspaper out of nowhere, and go to see what it's all about." And gutsy they were.

Each of us shared a piece of his or her journey and learned a little more about the devastations of long-term unemployment. We wondered about the human waste and pain in projections for seven to eight percent unemployment in this country into the 1980s and pondered the millions of lives disrupted, not a few broken. We shared what was breaking in our lives: the losses. We explored what was opening up in our lives: the learnings. On the last day we exchanged knowledge of resources and considered how we might help one another.

At lunch, as we were saying goodby, a woman stood and said, "I know what it's like to be alone on Christmas, and it's no good. You are all welcome at my house Christmas Eve or Day. If you call ahead you can be sure of getting something to eat, but in any case you'll be welcome." When asked to express on an evaluation sheet what was the most valuable part of the time together, participants wrote:

> I was able to identify with others and this in itself made me feel less isolated.

> The realization that I am not alone.

> The affirmation that my condition has not, for those present, detracted from my okayness.

> The absence, even for this short time, of harassment.

> Acceptance of the fact that there is no disgrace in being unemployed.

> Knowing that others have experienced the same fears, angers, and that I am not alone.

A man wrote, "I now realize that to leave the past allows me to enter the future. I feel better about my fellow journeyers as a result of being here." A woman wrote, "Being skeptical by nature of anything that smacks of 'instant intimacy' I am touched, even awed, at the fact that twenty-one strangers could in so short a time create a family in the best sense of that concept: supportive, non-judgmental and loving."

My heart smiled even as it ached through those days. It was as though the kingdom of God were happening before our eyes. It was like that story Jesus told about someone who invited his usual crowd to a dinner party, but they couldn't come and made excuses. So the host opened his doors and brought people in off the streets until his house was filled. Our house at Kirkridge was filled those days with "street people," people willing to make a blind journey to a strange little farmhouse hidden in a valley. I grinned to myself and thought, "Yes, these are my people, and I am theirs. These are the people I'm going home with. This is what the journey is all about."

Lots of good things came out of that first event for unemployed people. We touched a chord in our constituency. Our people were glad we had offered free hospitality to strangers. Letters and checks came in to help. We saw that we had discovered how to make "the unemployment connection." We had found a way to connect with unemployed people out there through a tiny ad in a paper. So we held a second event and a third and found ourselves developing a ministry with unemployed people. With adequate funding we could develop job counseling and referral but are currently unable to do so.

A serendipity is that letters and small gifts came from some people in that first group to help with the next groups. A few of those people came back to Kirkridge and became involved with us on a continuing basis. Strangers become friends! Our consciousness has been raised about the human devastation involved in long-term unemployment. We realize that our economic system has a defect in that it "must" throw off millions of unemployed people consistently. Fresh energy has been generated in us to work for creative change in our system toward economic justice for all, not just most of our people. We see that most people are out of work not because they aren't willing to work or look for a job hard enough, but because there just aren't enough jobs, or enough jobs that fit the skills and training of these people. We believe the Spirit is whispering to us in the broken lives of these unemployed stranger-friends. They are, in their anguish and anger, special spokespeople for the Spirit, calling us to work for that economic justice which is yet to be, that real homeland for humanity of which we now have only glimpses.

Turn with me to another page in the human family album. There are eighty-five people gathered around the hearth at the Kirkridge Lodge. A mix of clergy/laity, men/women, young/old, black/white, Protestant/Catholic, and straight/gay. This was an event on the theme Gay and Christian. It was for gay people, their relatives and friends, and those in the church who wanted to develop a more effective ministry with gay people. Our hope was to provide a safe and anonymous place where Christians who are gay could share their faith and sexual pilgrimage, explore the integration of their faith and life style, confront those personal and social dilemmas arising out of their gay orientation in a predominantly straight society. We also wanted to enable parents, spouses, children, and friends of gay people a caring environment in which to hear about and better understand the gay experience.

The event was promoted through our usual communication channels. The response was overwhelming. The event filled up within weeks of being announced, and a large waiting list developed. The need touched was immense and, as we were to discover, filled with anguish and anger. We listened to Jesuit scholar and priest John McNeill, author of one of the major new books in the field, *The Church and the Homosexual,* explore the familiar scriptural passages and issues. (As Christians we want to know what Jesus said about this matter. In fact, it appears that Jesus said absolutely nothing about homosexuality anywhere in the New Testament, so we cannot base our opinions directly on his teaching.) We heard about gay people losing their jobs, not being able to get housing, and in other ways having their civil rights denied them. We worshiped, prayed, argued, shared. It was the first time Cindy and I had been in a primarily gay ambience. There was some curiosity and a bit of apprehension. But soon we discovered, as people usually do when they find themselves in a milieu different from their typical experience, that people are people, gay people are people like straight people, responsible and vital human beings. We felt very comfortable and came to care for this community of searching, struggling, hurting Christians. Participants described their feelings about the experience in these ways:

> Most valuable to me was the camaraderie and concern shown by the entire group in trying to find ways in which to help dispel the problem of homophobia.

> For me, after fifteen years of life in the closet this was my *first* real contact with Christian gays. I carry away with me a New Beginning, a New Hope, a New Life!

> I feel that I've come to better terms with myself and my sexual journey, and feel much more informed and supported.

> I worked through a personal problem of alienation in my religious life, with help of friends in my small group.

A parent of a gay person wrote, "Learning firsthand to know gays, their concerns, hurts, accomplishments was most valuable. I've had very little contact with the gay community prior to this event. The group worship was indescribably beautiful."

To consider the issue of homosexuality raises the broader issue of human sexuality. We are often fearful of and judgmental about that which we don't understand, that which confronts us and jars us with new questions and new learning. Two major reports on human sexuality appeared in 1977: one from the Roman Catholic church and one from the United Church of Christ. Both reports remind us that we look for the Spirit's leading on ethical (including sexual) questions to three sources of guidance: scripture, tradition, and the behavioral sciences—the latter is sometimes a needed corrective to the former two. Of course, there is diversity of opinion on this issue. Gay caucuses exist in every denomination; questions of ordination and theology are being explored. It will take years of patient and knowledgeable work in the churches to gather insight, alter attitudes, and work out just and caring theology and ethics. But a *central* part of the church's mission is to welcome strangers (Matthew 25:35), to set at liberty those who are oppressed (Luke 4:18), and to reconcile the alienated (2 Corinthians 5:18). Therefore, as Christ's disciples, we must minister with and to the gay people in our churches and communities. Jesus Christ calls his church to be a community where people can be honest with one another about their faith and life journeys, without fear of condemnation or exclusion. The church is not called to judge; that is God's prerogative. Perhaps we can become a community working for the day when people who are straight and gay, married and single, celibate and living together in some form of covenant can sit together at table in the kingdom of God and maybe even in those here-and-now signposts of that kingdom called churches. Once again, the Spirit is whispering to us in the oppressed lives of our gay stranger-friends, calling us to work for a sexual justice which we do not now understand, that real homeland for humanity of which we now have only glimpses.

Let's turn another page in our human family album. There were several hundred people gathered in the sanctuary of the New York Society for Ethical Culture on November 20, 1977. The occasion was an event called The Night of the Empty Chairs, a benefit on behalf of Amnesty International (A.I.), a worldwide human rights movement that works for the release of persons imprisoned anywhere for their race, religion or ideas and was the recipient of the Nobel Peace Prize for 1977. Participants included Joel Grey, Art Buchwald, Richard Widmark, Lauren Bacall, William Styron, Susan Sontag, Robert Penn Warren, Studs Terkel, Bishop Paul Moore, singer Paul Simon, Arthur Miller, and Leonard Bernstein.

A plain chair stood on a bare stage. Stealthy as a panther, a mute Joel Grey stalked the chair while his recorded voice spoke of the more than 500,000 prisoners of conscience being punished in more than 100 countries. Slowly, gingerly, Grey sat down in the empty chair. His act of taking the chair symbolized the fact that participants that night were going to sit in the empty chairs of their imprisoned colleagues by reading or singing lines written by them and that the audience was there to share this witness in presence and financial support.

It was heavy. Paul Simon said, "We can't really understand in this country where we are paid so well for our art." He then sang songs written anonymously in

Soviet labor camps and a song of his own about a musician ("his hands were gentle, his hands were strong") whose hands were broken in prison. Billie Allen read part of a poem, "If You Want To Know Me: Reflections on Life in Southern Africa," written by Zinziswa Mandela, the sixteen-year-old daughter of Nelson Mandela, a leader in the African National Council sentenced in 1964 to life imprisonment for "treason and sabotage." In her poem Zinziswa wrote to her father, whom she has not seen since she was three years old: "How I wish I could see you, to tell you that I love you and to bring you comfort." Bishop Paul Moore read a letter written by his colleague Donal R. Lamont, Roman Catholic bishop of Umtali in Rhodesia/Zimbabwe. Lamont was exiled for not reporting the giving of medicines from his mission hospital to someone who may have been a local guerrilla agent. Richard Widmark read a letter smuggled out of a Havana prison from Huber Matos to his wife and children. Matos was a journalist and teacher imprisoned by Castro in 1959. He wrote, "I now know that I will die in prison. I am sad not to see you again, but I am at peace. They have swords but we have songs." And at the last, Leonard Bernstein played a song on the piano, an exuberant, Zorba-like Greek song written by his exiled colleague, Mikis Theodorakis.

Surrounded by so great a cloud of witnesses, what can we do? We who remember former prisoners of conscience: Jeremiah, Jesus, Paul, Peter, Joan of Arc, John Bunyan, John Hus, Dietrich Bonhoeffer, Martin Luther King—we can do something to share their witness. We can adopt a prisoner of conscience, often on a vocational basis, through the offices of Amnesty International, 2112 Broadway, New York, N.Y. 10023. Or we can give money to A.I. Or we can choose to sit in the empty chair of someone in our city or profession whose voice has been silenced. I have chosen to sit in the empty chair of Father John McNeill, who was silenced by the Vatican in late 1977. He was forbidden to write or speak about the issues of sexuality or homosexuality. With the cooperation of several colleagues, I have sought to gather public support protesting his silencing. Whose chair will you choose to sit in? To whose witness will you give wings by your own witness? To which homeless wanderers will you whisper or shout the good news?

Once again the Spirit is whispering to us in the oppressed lives of our "prisoner of conscience" stranger-friends, calling us to work for that political justice which is yet to be, that real homeland for humanity of which we now have only glimpses. Someone, somewhere is straining to hear a familiar welcome.

Let's turn another page of our human family album. Here are fifteen people working at Kirkridge for three days with experienced counselors. They are sharing the pain, anger, and fear arising out of their being separated and divorced. They are trying to deal with their losses, the damage to their self-esteem, and their anger. They are taking initial steps to put their lives together again. Hundreds of divorced people in our Formerly Married events over the last five years have told us that the church has branded them as failures, damaged goods, disobedient sinners. As we realize the huge number of people experiencing divorce in our time, we discover the need for a fresh theological understanding of divorce. Many local churches are still embarrassed and uncomfortable with divorced people and simply ignore them in their programming. Yet, divorced people also are children of God, also redeemable. Indeed, they can teach us some things we need to know. They can tell us what it is like to be alone again, to seek shyly and painfully for new relationships, once again to expose oneself to vulnerability and the possibility of hurt. They can tell us what it is to blend families, to become commuter or visiting parents, to gain stepparents, brothers, sisters, uncles, aunts, grandparents, and to move into that extended family with its perils and promises. They can tell us about the resilience of children and the enrichment of personal development as well as about loss, damage, and pain. The fact is that there will be millions of people, young and old, in the next period of time who will know the divorced condition of parents, selves, relatives, friends, or children. So we need to search out a new theological understanding of divorce and to develop a ministry with divorced persons and their relatives and friends. We need to hear what the Spirit is saying to us in the significant fact of major numbers of people having this experience. The Spirit is no "respecter" of institutions: political, economic, religious, familial, even those defined in the Bible. The Spirit calls us to health, integrity, and compassion in our roles and relationships and moves us to whatever choices lead toward these outcomes.

When I went for the first time to the home of my new father-in-law, Cindy and I drove up to the house and got out of the car. Her father came out the door and waited for us on the doorstep—a white-haired eighty-year-old man. Cindy hugged her father, turned to look at me, and said to her father, "I want to introduce a special stranger to you." Whereupon he said, "He's no stranger!" and warmly shook my hand. Everybody—whatever his or her condition of singlehood or couplehood—needs to hear somebody saying, "He's no stranger!" The local church should be the outpost of such hospitality, a community where we can recognize and welcome our divorced and separated brothers and sisters. The church must be less concerned with condemnation and exclusion and more concerned with affirmation and hospitality. We need to recognize that health, courage, and responsibility may be as much involved in decisions toward a divorce as in decisions for maintaining a marriage. The Spirit is not locked in either corner; she flows freely toward a responsible tomorrow, calling us to work for that familial justice which is yet to be, that real homeland for humanity of which we now have only glimpses.

What other pages in our human family album matter especially to you? We could have a page for handicapped people, or perhaps the poor in our city or state, or prisoners in our criminal justice system, or migrant farmworkers, or mothers and children on welfare, or old people who are poor and sick? "Our people" are so many and so diverse!

As sisters and brothers of Abraham and Sarah we are all pilgrims on a faith journey. We have left the security of home and gone out not knowing where we are to go, risking failure, seeking a homeland, and, for now, living in tents. Because we are pilgrims on such a faith journey, we live in tents of perpetual adaptation. And where is God in all this? Is it possible that God really cares about *all* the children of humanity? Is it possible that God is with us on our journey?

Robert McAfee Brown reminded me recently of a colloquial translation of the familiar Christmas scripture, ". . . the Word became flesh and dwelt among us" (John 1:14a). It was "God pitched his tent among us." What great news! God is a pilgrim God on a faith journey. God left the security of invulnerability to join our journey, risking failure, not knowing what would happen, seeking to bring all humanity, and indeed all creation, together in unity. God made himself accessible to us when he pitched his tent among us in Jesus. After sending messages over many centuries through many messengers, God came to us in person in the Jesus journey.

Creation (a star and animals) and humanity (parents, workers, gifted searchers) journeyed to the place of Jesus' birth. Beasts and angels were present. There being no room in the inn, Jesus was born in a stable, a temporary shelter, a tent. God *demonstrated* what Jesus would declare: that we must become like a child if we would see the kingdom of Spirit. So the Father/Mother became a child; the Creator became a creature. God pitched his tent among us.

Jesus lived in tents, with no place to lay his head. He left home to go on the road with strange good news of God's love for sinners and ordinary people. He journeyed to Jerusalem seeking a homeland for humanity, and there his tent was destroyed by the righteous elites. But the Jesus journey went on. He met two friends on the road to Emmaus, Saul on the road to Damascus, and countless others down the centuries. He meets you and me on the roads where we live and work this very day. Jesus journeys with us whenever we pitch our tents toward justice and peace.

Our hearts leap up when we behold a tent-pitcher on the earth. The gospel shouts the great joy that God has pitched his tent among us! The good news is not only that we believe in God, but that God believes in us still; not only that we hope in God, but that God's hope for us is undimmed; not only that we love God, but that God loves us without condition or ending.

God has thrown in his lot with us. He lives with us in tents of perpetual adaptation, seeking a homeland on earth as it is in heaven. God is going home with us. We are going home with our people. We journey in community, and yet, we walk alone.

We are going home to ourselves. Going home to ourselves means accepting the contours of our lives. Contours are limits, constraints, realities, givens. A fundamental contour for all of us is our home place. Curtis Harnack writes:

> Soon it'll be time for my annual visit to the home place, the Iowa farm 40 miles northeast of Sioux City where I grew up. . . . For 30 years I've been making the pilgrimage from various parts of the country, each time telling myself most likely this'll be the last. . . . Ownership of worked land holds people in one place longer than otherwise, and there are hundreds in the hometown region I'm acquainted with. Relatives and neighbors will have me in for a meal, setting a full table: home-grown food from the roast beef and potatoes to the apple pie. I'll observe the differences since last time— how the young have grown, the old aged; hear who got married; learn of births, deaths, good fortune and disaster. Like counting the rings on the stump of a felled tree, I'll determine how much margin to allot the past year. Nobody will find it odd that I should be interested in keeping up these primal connections. I'll be asked, "Where're you at now?" and what am I doing, what sort of job? After these preliminaries it'll be possible for me to find out about them, and myself in relation to them. . . . This former country life of mine and my current urban existence are joined in an instant and I feel whole. . . . We're adept at pulling up stakes, settling anew, becoming someone else, with different speech,

appearance and no baggage of personal history anywhere in evidence. But we never can be—in the deepest sense— anybody than we always were from the very beginning. I'm one of the rare individuals still with a physical home place to connect to, and I find it nourishing to be in proximity to a still-valid part of me once a year.[3]

I don't have a home place to which I can make pilgrimage now and then, a place where past and present can join together in an instant, a place of primal connections where I can touch sacred soil and know I am at the center once again. For many of us the home place has long since been wiped out by bulldozer or lost connections or sadness to which we do not want to return.

Others of us are still living in our home place. Richard Moore, a young friend of mine now seventeen years old, had some serious operations on his back and for several years had to spend much of his time at home. He writes "I used to feel somewhat stagnated by living here and being relatively confined to Columbus, Ohio. I'm finding more and more, however, that I really love it here. A few years ago, I named my room 'Tranquility Base' and began to look at it as my base of exploration—my centering place— just as Tranquility Base was the base of new exploration for the Apollo 11 astronauts. I'm realizing now that this 'base' is really my own personal retreat center, a place for self-exploration. This may not be the most exciting place in the world to live, but it has become beautiful to me just through the process of living and growing here." Many of us are working to make the place where we live such a home place, a place of centering and self-exploration, a

---

[3] Curtis Harnack, "Home," *The New York Times*, Aug. 28, 1977, p. E17.

place that to us has become beautiful simply by our living and loving there.

Some of us are city folk, mountaineers, countrypersons, islanders.

> I was searching for something on an island. Here people lived close to the earth, close to the sea, close to that which is natural and predetermined for us. The distinctive mark of the people I met, when the tourists had left at the end of the summer, was their simplicity. None of these men and women, I felt, could ever be humbled. They lived in harmony with their own selves, with everything that was good and evil in them. No outsiders could point at them and make them feel inferior. People who had trust in their place on earth. They were far from uncomplicated, nor without demands, hatreds and aggressions. But they had pride, a dignity which they allowed no one to crush. They had roots which had been lodged in the same piece of earth their entire lives. Many old people have that. They have renounced pretensions, dropped the false dream, stopped the mad rush. They, too, are islanders in our society. The way children are. People who don't care to keep the mask and the facade in order. Who dare to show who they are. Islanders. The ones who live their thoughts. Even thoughts that may not be so remarkable. From some of them emanates a feeling of security, a feeling of simple security, which may be the dignity of the heart.[4]

God has pitched his tent with us. He lives with us in tents as islanders, close to the sea, or on mountainsides or city streets. I want a home place where I can live in harmony with the good and evil in me, whose earth I trust, where I can live my thoughts, abide in simple

---

[4]Liv Ullmann, *Changing*, p. 120.

security, knowing that there I will die and be buried one day.

I'm aware of wanting such a place. I grew up in Minnesota, spent two years in the Navy in the United States and overseas, then seven years being educated in the East and another year in England. I have since spent twenty years in pastorates in Ohio and Pennsylvania and four years on a mountainside in Pennsylvania. I do not own a house or my own plot of land. I'm lonely for land of my own. When I made a new will this year, I wondered about arrangements for my burial. I knew that I wanted to be cremated, but where should the ashes be deposited? It came to me that I want the ashes of my body scattered along the shores of Glen Lake in Michigan, where my parents own land and cottages. I have made nearly annual pilgrimage there for twenty-eight years now. It is my only primal homeland connection. One day I will be part owner with my brothers and sister. I have so ordered it in my will, and I feel content.

Going home to ourselves means accepting the contours of our lives. Not that we don't want to change what should and can be changed, but that we become willing and able to accept what cannot be changed and to live with those realities. We all are offered a human community of people with whom to struggle for today's maturity and tomorrow's transformation. Our human muddle is the context for the creation of our home place. Bonhoeffer reminds us that going home means to accept the reality of our particular "bunch" of people and to stop fantasizing that they are or might become some other bunch of people. "Innumerable times a whole Christian community has broken down because it had sprung from a dream wish. . . .God's grace speedily shatters such dreams. . . . He who loves his dream of community more than . . . community itself becomes a destroyer of the latter, even though his personal intentions may be ever so honest and earnest and sacrificial."[5] Going home to ourselves means accepting the contours of our lives.

And, going home to ourselves means accepting the contours of ourselves. Such a going home takes the years of our lives to achieve if it is ever achieved. Self-acceptance comes slowly and painfully. There is a straining, reaching, yearning about youth which is appropriate to that time in our lives, but it becomes increasingly counterproductive and dissatisfying as we grow up during our middle years. In a whole page ad in *The New York Times, Playboy* featured a young architect named John Bradley Springer. He said, "I wish there were 70 minutes in every hour, 25 hours in every day and 8 days in every week. . . . When I give it's usually 110% of myself. . . . My career is on the threshold of skyrocketing. I can feel it. I know it. I'm good. I'm out there doing it, working harder than ever. I'm playing harder than ever, too. Until last year, I hadn't climbed a mountain since the Sierra Nevada back when I was in high school. Now I'm climbing again."[6]

He certainly is. Perhaps the time will come for him as it has for me, when walking on the level is enough, when sixty minutes, twenty-four hours, and seven days are enough, when it's enough to give all or part of myself in a given relationship, when there's a true ease of work and play in life. We are living our way toward completion of

---

[5] Dietrich Bonhoeffer, *Life Together* (New York: Harper & Row, 1954), pp. 26–27.

[6] *The New York Times,* Nov. 15, 1977, p. M36.

our responsibilities. In Saul Bellow's novel *Mr. Sammler's Planet*, Sammler goes to see his friend Elya Gruner, who has just died. He beholds the face of his dead friend, and prays.

> Remember, God, the soul of Elya Gruner, who, as willingly as possible and as well as he was able, and even to an intolerable point, and even in suffocation and even as death was coming was eager . . . to do what was required of him. At his best this man was much kinder than at my very best I have ever been, or could ever be. He was aware that he must meet, and he did meet—through all the confusion and degraded clowning of this life through which we are speeding—he did meet the terms of his contract. The terms which, in his inmost heart, each man knows. As I know mine. As all know. For that is the truth of it—that we all know, God, that we know, that we know, we know, we know.[7]

At fifty-two I am beginning to know the terms of my contract. I have not always lived up to those terms. On occasion I have broken some of them. Much of the time I have not fully known what they were. But as I come into my own in the second half of my life, I begin to know as I have been known. I want to meet the terms of my contract. Even as I have been much engaged in outer work in my life all these years, now I realize I have inner work to do as well. And I begin to understand that old age is a good time, an appropriate time, for some of this inner work. Abraham Heschel once said, "Old age is a major challenge to the inner life. . . . Old age involves the problem of what to do with privacy. . . . There are alleys in the soul where man walks alone . . . ways that do not lead to society, a world of privacy that shrinks from the public eye. Life

---

[7]Saul Bellow, *Mr. Sammler's Planet* (New York: Viking, 1970), p. 313.

comprises not only arable productive land but also mountains of dreams, an underground of sorrow, towers of yearning."[8]

We are wise if we do some of our dreaming all along the way, if we are in touch with our sorrow when we suffer loss, if we pay attention to our yearnings when they rise within our hearts. So our self-knowledge might grow with our years. So we might make of old age a formative time when we seek and find insights we missed along the way because we were so preoccupied. We might seek the wisdom we ignored. We might see through those inbred deceptions required of us to be successful and productive. We might find a deeper understanding and compassion for people with whom we no longer have to compete, whom we need not fear anymore. Heschel continued, "Wisdom is the substance upon which the inner security of the old will forever depend. But the attainment of wisdom is the work of a lifetime. Old men (and women) need a vision, not only recreation. Old men (and women) need a dream not only a memory. It takes three things to attain a sense of significant being: God, a soul, and a Moment. And the three are always here. Just to be is a blessing. Just to live is holy."[9]

Attaining a sense of significant being.

Meeting the terms of our contract.

Accepting the contours of ourselves.

Accepting ourselves.

That last is the hardest part. Because it's hard for us to accept a gift, undeserved, unearned, just freely given.

---

[8]Abraham J. Heschel, "To Grow in Wisdom," *The Christian Ministry* (March 1971), pp. 31–37, address given at White House Conference on Aging.

[9]*Ibid.*

Accepting the fact that we are accepted, that God is not ashamed of us.

No wonder we respond to that shameless lover, the Man of La Mancha. Remember how Don Quixote treats the kitchen woman, Aldonza, as though she were a queen, and even gives her a new name, Dulcinea! At first she reacts with the crude cynicism of her exploited years, saying he's after what all men are after. But through the hard shell of her bitterness and rejection, he keeps affirming her nobility, her virtue, until she asks wonderingly,

> "Why do you do these things?"
> "What things, my lady?"
> "These ridiculous . . . the things you do!"
> "I hope to add some measure of grace to the world."
> "The world's a dungheap and we are maggots that crawl on it!"
> "My lady knows better in her heart."[10]

Slowly, as in disbelief that there was one who could know her through and through and love her still and all, tough, hardened Aldonza lets her heart open just a chink to Don Quixote. She begs him to see her as she really is—in her own eyes, a worthless woman. She tries to fend off his gentle words, but cannot. Her anger melts in the face of his tenderness, releasing her sorrow and hurt. Her defenses gone, she can scarcely bear her fresh vulnerability. Nor can you and I. Love penetrates armor that can resist condemnation year after year. At the end of the play, as Don Quixote lies dying, confused, and doesn't remember people or their names, we can understand why Aldonza pleads with him to remember her name. He says,

---

[10] Dale Wasserman, *Man of La Mancha* (New York: Random House, 1966), p. 85.

"Is it so important?" And she says through her tears, "Everything. My whole life. You spoke to me and everything was—different! . . . You looked at me! And you called me by another name! Dulcinea . . . Dulcinea. . . . When you spoke the name an angel seemed to whisper— Dulcinea . . . Dulcinea. . . ."[11]

Colonies of heaven happen on earth whenever people hear their names called and know as they are known. The Gospel shouts the good news that God is not ashamed to be our God. God knows us through and through and loves us still and all. God is with us as we go home to ourselves.

Going home. Homeland earth, our own precious precarious earth-star being hurled and whirled through space, a tiny light in the vast darkness. Archibald MacLeish wrote, "To see the earth as it truly is, small and blue and beautiful in that eternal silence where it floats, is to see ourselves as riders on the earth together, brothers on that bright loveliness in the eternal cold, brothers who know now they are truly brothers." Brothers and sisters of Abraham and Sarah riding on the earth together, but riding where and to what finally? If our homeland earth is whirling on its own immense journey toward cosmic death and rebirth, how do we conceive our ending and beginning again? God is preparing for us a city.

> Then I saw a new heaven and a new earth; the first heaven and the first earth had disappeared now, and there was no longer any sea. I saw the holy city, and the new Jerusalem, coming down from God out of heaven, as beautiful as a bride all dressed for her husband. Then I heard a loud voice call from the throne, "You see this city? Here God lives among men. He will make his home among them; they shall be his

---

[11] *Ibid.*, p. 119.

people, and he will be their God; his name is God-with-them. He will wipe away all tears from their eyes; there will be no more death, and no more mourning or sadness. The world of the past has gone." Then the One sitting on the throne spoke: "Now I am making the whole of creation new."

Revelation 21:1–5, JB

The gospel shouts the good news that God is making his home with us, that we are homeless wanderers no more. We are not yet home, but we are going home. Going home to that homecoming banquet where elder brother and prodigal son, father and son, mother and daughter, exile and stranger, man and woman, white and black, East and West, Arab and Jew, poor and rich, lion and lamb will sit down together in peace. The biblical word of new creation, of resurrection, suggests that all our history—personal and communal, over all the aeons, over all the earth and throughout the entire cosmos—is not lost or forgotten. Rather, all is gathered up, restored, offered, celebrated, shared, brought into communion. As in the Nicene Creed, "I look for the resurrection of the dead and the life of the world to come." Yes, I look and keep on looking, and sometimes I think I glimpse it from afar. And if someone tells me that "eternity is in an hour" and that homeland heaven is available right now on homeland earth, I will nod and celebrate and enjoy. But I will still wonder about the mystery which is to come—the mystery in which we shall all be changed, the mystery of that communion of the saints streaming in the gates of home when no one will be on the outside, ever again.